D0755296

PUBLISHED BY TURRE PUBLISHING,

A DIVISION OF TURRE LEGAL LTD.

Aleksanterinkatu 17, 6th floor, Helsinki, FI-00100, Finland
http://pub.turre.com/

Copyright © 2007 Herkko Hietanen, Ville Oksanen and
Mikko Välimäki. First Edition. Some Rights Reserved.

Cover and layout: Lauri Ahonen.

This book is licensed under the terms of Creative Commons
Attribution-NonCommercial-NoDerivs 2.5 license available from
http://creativecommons.org/licenses/by-nc-nd/2.5/

Accordingly, you are free to copy, distribute, display, and perform
the work under the following conditions:

(1)   you must give the original author credit,
(2)   you may not use this work for commercial purposes, and
(3)   you may not alter, transform, or build upon this work.

ISBN: 978-952-99834-0-7

Printed in Helsinki by Multiprint.

Herkko Hietanen | Ville Oksanen | Mikko Välimäki

Community
Created Content

Law, Business and Policy

TURRE LEGAL

FOREWORD

Figure 1.

Time magazine chose You as the person of the year 2006.

"One-to-many" media culture is changing gradually because of the Internet's end-to-end architecture where anyone can send and receive. The Internet has changed the way people experience content. They do not only passively consume but they also remix, mash up, create and share. Capturing the wealth of networked producers and creators may turn out to be one of the biggest factors that will help to increase our society's productivity during this century. "User created content", "social software" and "web 2.0" may be the hottest buzzwords of the Internet economy today. They all refer to community created content.

The value of professionally produced content is not disappearing. Amateur content, in many cases, complements professional content. Citizen journalism comments and offers different angles to stories. Social networking sites help users to filter interesting material out of the vast amount of information on the Internet. Designing services that harness the wealth of their users' creativity is not trivial. Finding a balance between exclusive copyright and open has turned out to be a delicate task.

This book is written to help its readers to understand the legal, business and policy issues affecting community created content. The aim was to write a handy reference and a useful overview of a complex subject. Main emphasis is on the legal underpinnings of community created content. The book also describes users' different motives of sharing their works. Several case studies help to illustrate how businesses can adapt to accommodate community created content.

The book is based on a commission from "PARTECO - To Participatory Economy and Beyond" -research project coordinated by the Hypermedia Laboratory at the University of Tampere. The project is funded by the Finnish Funding Agency for Technology and Innovation (Tekes) and the following companies: Aina Group, A-lehdet, Tuotantoyhtiö Energia, Ericsson, Professia, COSS - The Finnish Centre for Open Source Solutions, and Mediamaisteri Group. The authors wish to thank the researchers at the University of Tampere and especially Katri Lietsala for constructive comments and cooperation during the writing of this book.

The writing of this book was divided between the authors but the end result is a joint whole. The authors are also jointly responsible for any errors.

Finally, a legal disclaimer is in place. This book is written by three lawyers who also consult clients on open content issues. The book includes several fictive case illustrations with "legal advice" included. Laws and legal interpretations change. New case law is made. Copyright law interpretation must be done on a case-by-case basis. For those reason the authors do not take any responsibility for the advice given in this book. Please consult your lawyer before applying anything presented in this book.

Helsinki, January 10, 2007

Herkko Hietanen, Ville Oksanen and Mikko Välimäki

1. Introduction

"Think Woodstock, without the mud, and
where the audience makes the music."

– Lessig blog 29.1.2005

Community created content poses many challenges for service providers and users. The focus of this book is on the legal issues. Obviously, this kind of book cannot cover all relevant areas of law that affect community created content. Thus, it has been necessary to make selections and limitations. Partly the selection is based on the intuitive understanding of the authors and partly on the fictive case studies submitted by the researchers at the University of Tampere.

The authors of this book believe that the most crucial questions in community created content are the usage rules for the content itself. All creative content is covered by copyright. This also means that copyright licenses define in most cases how services can utilize the content submitted by users. There are of course situations where copyright is not the main issue. Sometimes the content can be illegal based on criminal law. Other relevant areas of the law, which are briefly covered in this book, include data protection and editorial liability for the service provider.

Although the book mainly discusses legal issues, the authors want to stress that laws are never applied in abstract. In practice, legal regulation limits the operating possibilities of community content services. With that in mind, this book also discusses different businesses that have utilized community created content. And finally, based on the legal review and business studies, the book makes forward-looking policy recommendations. Having better laws and other norms in place makes better community created content services possible as well.

In this book, community created content is approached from the perspectives of two actors:

1. A service provider that utilizes community created content. The authors have had in mind a Finland-based service, which must decide what kind of copyright licenses and other usage policies it applies. What options does the service have and how do given decisions impact its operating possibilities?

2. A productive user of a content community. A community service does not exist without users. How can users best help the services without losing the legal control to their creative contributions? How do users see different copyright licenses and other usage policies?

The book is structured in three main parts. The first and longest part (chapters 2-3) is legal. It starts from the basics of copyright law and other relevant legislation that applies to community created content services. Then, the book comments on different usage rules for community created content services. Emphasis is in the details of most popular open content copyright licenses. In addition, the book briefly covers the main points in terms of service contracts and privacy policies. Mikko Välimäki was mainly responsible for this part of the book.

The second part (chapters 4-5) has a business perspective. It discusses different community content business models from both conceptual and practical perspectives. Practical business cases illustrate how different companies have been able to utilize open content licensing and other tools to create successful services that utilize community created content. Herkko Hietanen was the author mainly responsible for this part of the book.

The third part (chapter 6) focuses on policy. It discusses issues ranging from the details copyright law to collecting societies and the interplay between different licensing projects. Ville Oksanen was the author mainly responsible for this part of the book.

2. Law and Content

2.1 INTRODUCTION

The approach taken towards legal issues in this book is partly international, partly national. True, all laws applied in a given country are
national. However, most Internet services are truly global. Users can
submit and retrieve material to community content services in principle
from any location in the world. Sometimes the laws of a given country
cover all services accessible to its citizens. This also means that those
services must also have a basic understanding of the laws of different
jurisdictions where relevant.

Copyright is perhaps the most internationalized regime of private
law. This makes it also natural to discuss copyright from an international perspective in this book. The book mainly refers to international
copyright treaties and European Union legislation with comparisons to
United States doctrine where applicable. Details of for example the Finnish copyright law are omitted. Finnish copyright law follows today rather
closely the European doctrine.

In contrast, criminal law remains as one of the most national areas
of law. Only Convention on Cybercrime harmonizes some particular
criminal policy issues like child porn internationally. Thus, in sections
discussing crimes such as privacy intrusion and hate speech, the book
refers extensively to Finnish law. As noted, the perspective taken is that
of a Finland-based service provider.

2.2 COPYRIGHT

2.2.1 Evolving global law

For over a century, international treaties have guaranteed the global existence of copyright and author's rights. Most important of them is the Berne Convention. Compared to many other areas of private law, copyright can be considered international by nature. This does not mean that there would be something like "international copyright act" in existence. Individual countries that are members of the World Intellectual Property Organization (WIPO) – practically almost all countries – have agreed to write their national copyright laws according to the minimum standards set in the treaties. In Europe, European Union has further enacted a number of copyright directives that harmonize many details of copyright law left open in the international treaties.

According to copyright law, the authors of works such as text, pictures, music and video are given a set of exclusive rights to govern the publication and copying of their works. This also means that one needs a prior permission to publish or copy a work that is under copyright. Without permission, one can be liable to copyright infringement, which can be enforced in any country with a copyright law in par with the minimum international standards.

Copyright law is not without limits, however. First, if the requirements for copyright protection are not fulfilled, the work remains in the public domain. For example, copyright does not cover mere ideas but only creative expression. Further, the term of copyright is generally limited to 70 years after the death of the author. In sum, all works end up in public domain. This means that every work can be one distant day used freely for any purpose including publication and copying without prior permission.

Second, copyright law itself includes a set of user rights (or exceptions to exclusive rights). Depending on jurisdiction, the user rights can be defined either openly as in the United States or through a closed list as in the European Union. They generally include for example private use, citation and parody. In other words, one does not need permission for example to make a citation from a copyrighted work.

The edges of copyright are in constant change. As new technical ways to use copyrighted works are invented, there is often need to clarify whether a certain use is under copyright or not. When the Internet became popular, it was for example clarified that access providers do not infringe copyright even though they route and transmit copyrighted works. In this kind of situations, legislators or courts need to consider policy arguments both favoring and disfavoring the regulation of a certain new use. Arguments favoring the extension of copyright vary typically from moral ethics (e.g. private property) to economic logic (e.g. incentive theory). Arguments in favor of limiting copyright vary from cultural needs (e.g. education) to societal reasons (e.g. disabled persons) and economic logic (e.g. competition).

2.2.2 Work

The object of copyright is defined in law as "a work". In more legal language, the concept of work defines the subject matter of copyright. Depending on the perspective, one may say that copyright essentially "protects" or "restricts" certain uses of the work.

The main requirement for copyright is that the work is original and not merely copied. Originality is not defined in international treaties or in most national laws. It is usually agreed that an original work must be somewhat "new" and require an author's own creative effort. Further, the work must be expressive. Ideas and principles are not considered copyrightable.

Almost any type of work can qualify for copyright. Berne convention – the most relevant international copyright treaty – defines literary and artistic works subject to copyright as:

"   *...every production in the literary, scientific and artistic domain, whatever may be the mode or form of its expression, such as books, pamphlets and other writings; lectures, addresses, sermons and other works of the same nature; dramatic or dramatico-musical works; choreographic works and entertainments in dumb show; musical compositions with or without words; cinematographic works to which are assimilated works expressed by a process analogous to cinematography; works of drawing, painting, architecture, sculpture, engraving and lithography; photographic works to which are assimilated works expressed by a process analogous to photography; works of applied art; illustrations, maps, plans, sketches and three-dimensional works relative to geography, topography, architecture or science.*

The list above is not exhaustive. For example the Berne convention itself clarifies that member states can define whether applied art and industrial design are subject to copyright. Another treaty adds computer programs and original compilations of data to the list.

2.2.3 Authorship – individual and collective

In most cases, copyright belongs to the individual author. Only in limited cases the copyright may vest with the employer or a corporation. Major exceptions are the United States and United Kingdom, where the employer typically becomes the copyright holder by law. In most other countries employees transfer copyright through employment contracts. Further, copyright laws list specific types of works and specific rights where corporations may become the copyright holder directly by law. These include copyright to computer programs and "neighboring rights" such as performer's and sound recorder's rights to audiovisual works. If a corporation owns the copyright, the individual author can no longer make a licensing decision on his own.

If more than one author participates in the creation of a work, the copyright to the resulting work is shared ("joint authorship"). If for example two individuals write a paper together, the result is typically a joint work. In other words, co-authors become co-owners of the copyright. Unless otherwise agreed, the ownership ratios are typically shared equally. One then needs the permission from all authors of a joint work to license the work. An exception here is the United States where even one joint copyright holder can make the decision to use a non-exclusive license for the work. He must then compensate other authors for any profits.

If the contributions of individual authors are separate, then also copyright remains separate ("collective authorship"). If for example one adds to his paper a picture taken by another, the result is a collective work. Also editors of collective volumes may have the copyright to the collective whole while individual authors retain copyrights to their individual contributions. One typically needs again the permission of all copyright holders for the licensing of the whole work.

2.2.4 Exclusive rights – economic and moral

As already noted, copyright gives to the authors of original works a set of exclusive rights. The most important rights are:

1. Reproduction of the work ("right to copy"). Also the reproduction of modifications – including "translations, adaptations, arrangements" as defined in Berne convention – is treated as an exclusive right of the author. United States copyright law defines a separate right to prepare derivative works resulting in most cases with the same outcome.

2. Communication of the work to the public ("publication right"). This may be further realized through the distribution, rental, or lending of a copy, placing the work available to the public, or making a public performance or public display of the work.

As an important limitation, the distribution right covers only the first sale of a copy and, thus, it is possible to trade for example used books without copyright holder's explicit permission.

As time has passed and new technologies introduced, the set of exclusive rights has expanded to make sure that certain new uses of works are covered. The most recent addition was the right to place the work publicly available in a way that the members of the public can individually access the work. This right covers different "on-demand" content delivery methods on the Internet. Still, some uses remain controversial. It is for example unclear to what extent exclusive rights cover linking on the Internet. Probably links that "bring in" content from third party sources are covered but typical hyperlinks, which take the user to a new destination, are outside copyright.

License agreements typically define in detail the extent to which one is allowed to use a certain exclusive right. There are generally no restrictions to license, transfer or even waive any of these economic components of copyright.

An exception is moral rights, which are non-transferable. The most important moral rights – also based on Berne convention – are:

1. Right to be attributed as the author of the work ("paternity right").

2. Right to prohibit such modifications of the work, which could damage the author's honor or reputation ("integrity right")

As an important exception, United States copyright law recognizes moral rights only partially. It may be thus necessary to write specific license clauses for example to require attribution if the work is used in the United States.

2.2.5 Anti-circumvention of technological measures – DRM

WIPO Copyright Treaty, signed in 1996, established the international background for the anti-circumvention regulation of technological measures. These were introduced in US copyright law in 1998 and European copyright law through a directive in 2001. Depending on the perspective, one can say that the regulation of technological measures legally enforces "digital rights management" or "digital restrictions management" (DRM) systems. Article 11 of the WIPO Copyright Treaty states:

§   *Contracting Parties shall provide adequate legal protection and effective legal remedies against the circumvention of effective technological measures that are used by authors in connection with the exercise of their rights under this Treaty or the Berne Convention and that restrict acts, in respect of their works, which are not authorized by the authors concerned or permitted by law.*

WIPO Copyright Treaty clearly limits the enforceability of DRM only to the extent covered by copyright law. As an extension, national copyright laws may make it also possible to enforce such technological measures that cover non-copyrightable uses of a work or uses for which there are exceptions ("user rights"). This is argu-ably the situation at least in Europe. Thus, many commentators and activists have started to criticize that technological measures can be now used to extend copyright well beyond its previously bal-anced statutory scope.

2.2.6 User rights

Copyright is balanced through a set of exceptions to the exclusive rights. Berne convention generally allows exceptions to copying on the following basis, commonly called as the three-step-test:

§   *[exceptions to the right to copy are allowed in] ... certain special cases, provided that such reproduction does not conflict with a normal exploitation of the work and does not unreasonably preju-dice the legitimate interests of the author.*

Depending on perspective, one can also call these exceptions as "user rights" as is done in this book. Most jurisdictions have a closed list of user rights. The most important user rights, indepen-dent of jurisdiction, are:

1.   Private use. However, while private use can be done without authorization, for most private uses national copyright laws may require "fair compensation" to be paid. These are usually real-ized through levies based on recording capacity. Thus one could characterize private use as a user right with "strings attached."

2.   Certain public uses such as parody, news reporting, teaching and citation. Copyright laws require typically no compensation to be paid for these uses, the main exception being teaching.

United States copyright law has a different approach to user rights. It has an open-ended fair use doctrine, which is based on statutory four-factor test:

1.   The purpose and character of the use, including whether such use is of commercial nature or is for nonprofit educational purposes;

2.   The nature of the copyrighted work;

3.   The amount and substantiality of the portion used in relation to the copyrighted work as a whole; and

4.   The effect of the use upon the potential market for or value of the copyrighted work.

Although the doctrine is only found in the United States copyright law, one can consider practical cases where a certain use is accepted as fair but there is no clearly listed user right available elsewhere. One can then perhaps find support to interpret a listed right in accordance with the fair use doctrine. For example, there is currently no listed user right that covers search engines without doubt.

2.3 OTHER RELEVANT LEGISLATION

2.3.1 Criminal law: privacy, defamation, hate crimes, child pornography etc.

Compared to copyright law, criminal law has been traditionally rather national law. As of today, most crimes that affect community created content services remain strictly national law. The only applicable major international convention is Convention on Cybercrime, signed in 2001. However, there are ongoing initiatives aiming at more harmonization especially in name of the fight against terrorism so the situation may change in the near future.

In general, most countries criminalize the invasion of privacy. For example the Finnish penal code, chapter 24, section 8, states:

§   *(1) A person who unlawfully*
(1) through the use of the mass media, or
(2) in another manner publicly spreads information, an insinuation or an image of the private life of another person, so that the act is conducive to causing that person damage or suffering, or subjecting that person to contempt, shall be sentenced for an invasion of personal reputation to a fine or to imprisonment for at most two years.

As a general limitation, the invasion of privacy does not cover the evaluation of one's activities in public position including business, politics and science.

Most countries also criminalize defamation. Finnish penal code, chapter 24, section 9, states:

§ *(1) A person who*
(1) spreads false information or a false insinuation of another person so that the act is conducive to causing damage or suffering to that person, or subjecting that person to contempt, or
(2) makes a derogatory comment on another otherwise than in a manner referred to in subparagraph (1) shall be sentenced for defamation to a fine or to imprisonment for at most six months.

Section 10 adds that if the defamation "is committed by using the mass media or otherwise by making the information or insinuation available to a large number of people" the sentence can be up to two years in prison. As a general limitation, defamation does not cover appropriate criticism of one's activities in public position including business, politics and science.

Hate speech is criminalized in most European countries. It is worth noting, however, that the United States does not recognize hate speech at all as a crime. Convention of Cybercrime includes a separate "Additional Protocol to the Convention on Cybercrime, concerning the criminalisation of acts of a racist and xenophobic nature committed through computer systems" that sets the requirement for criminalization:

§   *Each Party shall adopt such legislative and other measures as may be necessary to establish as criminal offences under its domestic law, when committed intentionally and without right, the following conduct: distributing, or otherwise making available, racist and xenophobic material to the public through a computer system.*

Finland has signed the protocol and the Finnish penal code chapter 11, section 8, states:

§   *A person who spreads statements or other information among the public where a certain race, a national, ethnic or religious group or a comparable group is threatened, defamed or insulted shall be sentenced for ethnic agitation to a fine or to imprisonment for at most two years.*

Some countries including Finland also criminalize the distribution of violent or sexually obscene pictures (Finnish penal code, chapter 17: "Offences against public order"). Convention on Cybercrime requires signatories to specifically criminalize the production, offering, distributing, procuring and possessing child pornography through computer systems. Finally, some authoritarian countries criminalize political communications, which may undermine the government.

2.3.2 Editorial regulation of mass media

Many countries have editorial regulation of mass media that applies also to community created content services. In Finland, the Act on the Exercise of Freedom of Expression in Mass Media (460/2003) applies to various kind of "network publications" defined as "a set of network messages, arranged into a coherent whole comparable to a periodical from material produced or processed by the publisher, and intended to be issued regularly." The definition covers obviously for example various news sites and blogs, where users submit stories and an editor accepts them.

The act defines a set of obligations that apply to corporate publishers (but not private individuals):

1.   Publication is required to designate a "responsible editor" who must be 15 years or older, who is not in bankrupt, and whose competency has not been restricted.

2.   Publication is required to disclose information about itself including the identity of the publication, publication year, and the responsible editor

3.   Publication is required to store all the content published for at least 21 days unless it is clear that the content can not constitute a criminal offence

4.   Publication is required to publish a reply or correction to the content it has published. A request must be made in 14 days after the publication of the content in question. The request can be rejected with a valid reason.

Regarding liability, the act refers to penal code and general tort liability act. Further, the act defines editorial misconduct:

§ *If the responsible editor intentionally or negligently fails in an essential manner in his or her duty to manage and supervise editorial work, and the failure is conducive to the occurrence of an offence arising from the contents of a message provided to the public, and the offence occurs without him or her being considered the perpetrator or accomplice, the responsible editor shall be convicted of editorial misconduct and sentenced to a fine.*

The law also defines on what circumstances the authorities may demand taking material down from a publication or may confiscate the material. The former requires a separate decision from the court, which has to hear the publisher before making the decision. The latter is possible without getting a court order first. After the confiscation has been made, it has to be reviewed by the court in three days.

Finally, the law has a provision (section 16) on protecting the sources of news. The protection applies to all kinds of net publications including those provided by private persons. As a consequence, bloggers enjoy this protection that can be characterized exceptional in the global perspective.

2.3.3 Data protection

Most countries require those who build a database of users to keep all private user information confidential. Data protection is in general more strictly regulated in Europe compared to the United States and other regions. Thus, if a community content service follows European data protection regulation, it should do fine elsewhere as well.

Data protection directive (95/46/EC) defines possible purposes when personal data can be processed. If the user has not given his consent to process the data, there must in general be a legitimate reason. According to the directive, the user's consent is specifically needed if one collects "personal data revealing racial or ethnic origin, political opinions, religious or philosophical beliefs, trade-union membership, and the processing of data concerning health or sex life." The directive has a number of exceptions to these principles mainly covering public security, defense and the investigation of criminal offenses. The directive also gives to users the right to access the data, the right to know how the data is being used, where it was collected from, and to whom it is being given.

Finally, the directive obliges those who collect and process data to notify public authorities about their database. This can be in most cases done in a simple formal notification available on the Internet. The notification must include at least the following details as defined in article 19:

§   *(a) the name and address of the controller and of his representative,*
if any;
(b) the purpose or purposes of the processing;
(c) a description of the category or categories of data subject and of
the data or categories of data relating to them;
(d) the recipients or categories of recipient to whom the data might
be disclosed;
(e) proposed transfers of data to third countries;
(f) a general description allowing a preliminary assessment to be
made of the appropriateness of the measures taken pursuant to Ar-
ticle 17 to ensure security of processing."

2.3.4 Other intellectual property rights than copyright

Finally, one must take into account that community created content may infringe other third party intellectual property rights than copyright. Most obvious is trademark law, which does not allow confusing commercial use of the mark. Many companies have detailed trademark usage policies on their websites.

Also of note is that during the last few years, it has become possible to register parts of user interfaces such as small icons on websites under community design regulation in Europe.

2.4 LIABILITY AND REMEDIES

2.4.1 Direct and indirect liability

Regarding copyright, international treaties do not have much to say about liability and, hence, liability rules are part of national copyright laws. United States and European copyright laws differ substantially in the extent of copyright liability doctrines. Both treat the defined uses under exclusive rights without authorization as a (direct) copyright infringement. In addition, United States copyright law has three separate doctrines for indirect copyright liability: contributory liability, vicarious liability and active inducement liability. By comparison, in Europe only general doctrines of joint criminal liability may extent the liability for copyright infringement to indirect infringers.

Understandably, too extensive liability doctrines could undermine the development of new content services. In Europe, directive on certain legal aspects of information society services (2000/31/EC) defines in articles 12-14 situations where a third party is exempted from liability based on any law including copyright, defamation, hate speech etc. Covered services include technical data transfer and caching by Internet operators as well as all kind of "hosting" services including the provision of discussion forums and search engines. Regarding copyright, a general requirement is that the service provider has no control or actual knowledge of the possibly infringing activity. Further, the directive specifically says that there is no obligation to monitor a qualified service. A copyright holder can establish required knowledge by sending a take-down notice. In most respects similar rules apply in the United States as well.

Case study:

EDITORIAL LIABILITY FOR USER CREATED CONTENT

DESCRIPTION: There is a part in a magazine's webpage, which publishes only content created by the user community: text, pictures and video. Anyone can register and start creating content with the tools provided by the magazine. All community created content waits until magazine editors check whether the content is not against the law and whether it looks trustworthy. Editors have the power either to edit or publish the content as such. They can also check the information substance in the content and comment back to ask for clarifications before publishing.

All community created content worth publishing gets eventually published. Some of the most interesting contributions are shown on the magazine front page. Magazine does not pay for contributors when publishing takes place online. Only if the content is later published in the print version, does the author get compensated.

PROBLEM AND ADVICE: The problem here is, first, potential indirect liability for editors (and the magazine itself). If the editors would not review all submissions, they could claim they did not have actual knowledge of the content. They would be merely hosting it under their magazine's webpage.

Second, the editors might be even directly liable if they edit the content substantially and become co-authors. It is thus recommended that any editing is kept at bare minimum.

One additional way to mitigate the problem is to require all contributors to click through an assurance, where they state not to have copied the submission from elsewhere and they do not post any illegal content such as hate speech or illegal pornography. The flip side of the assurance is that there are potentially less contributors because of increasing risks. It may also fall short of releasing the editors from liability.

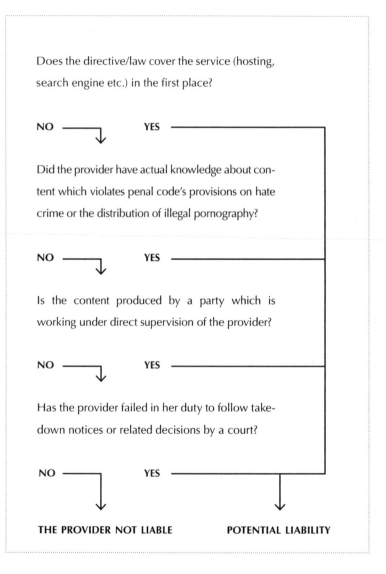

Does the directive/law cover the service (hosting, search engine etc.) in the first place?

NO ——⌐   YES ——
      ↓

Did the provider have actual knowledge about content which violates penal code's provisions on hate crime or the distribution of illegal pornography?

NO ——⌐   YES ——
      ↓

Is the content produced by a party which is working under direct supervision of the provider?

NO ——⌐   YES ——
      ↓

Has the provider failed in her duty to follow take-down notices or related decisions by a court?

NO ——⌐   YES ——
      ↓   ↓

THE PROVIDER NOT LIABLE   **POTENTIAL LIABILITY**

Figure **2.**

Finnish law's process for liability exemption based on the directive.

2.4.2 Remedies

As most criminal offences discussed above define remedies in themselves, the book concentrates here on remedies from copyright infringement. Those can be divided in two main categories: monetary compensation and criminal penalties. There can be some additional sanctions as well. As with liability, remedies are part of national law.

In Europe, the directive on the enforcement of intellectual property rights (2004/48/EC) requires that the copyright holder is entitled to damages caused by willful infringers:

§   *Member States shall ensure that the competent judicial authorities, on application of the injured party, order the infringer who knowingly, or with reasonable grounds to know, engaged in an infringing activity, to pay the rights holder damages appropriate to the actual prejudice suffered by him/her as a result of the infringement.*

The directive does not set a requirement to pay damages for non-willful infringers. However, at least "fair compensation" is available in most of the EU-member states:

§   *Where the infringer did not knowingly, or with reasonable grounds know, engage in infringing activity, Member States may lay down that the judicial authorities may order the recovery of profits or the payment of damages, which may be pre-established.*

The monetary compensation may be calculated based on actual damages suffered by the copyright holder or a lump sum considering potentially lost license sales. Further, the directive has a wide range of other tools for copyright holders including:

1. Destruction of the goods infringing an intellectual property right;

2. Total or partial closure, on a permanent or temporary basis, of the establishment used primarily to commit the offence;

3. A permanent or temporary ban on engaging in commercial activities;

4. Publication of judicial decisions.

Remedies differ to some extent in the United States. Instead of fair compensation, US copyright law defines specific sums of "statutory damages" that can be anything between $ 750 and $ 30 000 per infringed work based on the facts of the case. For willful infringement statutory damages can count up to $ 150 000 per work. US copyright holders must register their work with the Copyright Office to be able to claim for statutory damages.

Criminal sanctions are also available. European Union is currently contemplating a proposal titled "Amended proposal for a Directive of the European Parliament and of the Council on criminal measures aimed at ensuring the enforcement of intellectual property rights" (COM/2006/0168 final). The key section about the scope is currently defined as follows:

§   *"Member States shall ensure that all intentional infringements of an intellectual property right on a commercial scale, and attempting, aiding or abetting and inciting such infringements, are treated as criminal offences."*

The formulation excludes non-commercial and non-willing violations but on the other hand it includes aiding or abetting and inciting, which broaden the scope considerably. The sanctions for these violations are proposed to include 1) fines and the confiscation of the object, instruments and products stemming from infringements for both natural and legal persons and 2) prison sentences to individuals.

To compare, the United States No Electronic Theft Act has a wider scope covering also non-commercial infringement. It defines somewhat stricter criminal sanctions including prison sentences up to five years, fines up to $ 250 000, and also increased statutory damages.

3. Usage Rules for Community Created Content

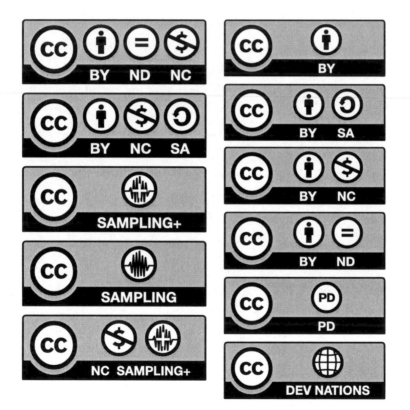

Figure 3.

Creative Commons licence buttons.

3.1   INTRODUCTION

Next, this book reviews different usage rules that take into account the laws discussed in the previous chapter. Much of the community created copyrighted content is licensed with open content licenses. Every day numerous new blogs are opened, new pictures uploaded and millions of lines of text written under the principles of open content licenses. Hundreds of millions of people create and use this content every day. Authors have chosen an explicit copyright license to permit users to copy the content and distribute it to other users, in most cases free-of-charge.

One of the main principles of copyright is that one needs authorization – usually against payment – to use a copyrighted work. Obviously, community created content builds on the principles of free use of the works of others. Before the Internet, public domain (works whose copyright had either expired or never existed) as well as copyright exceptions were the main sources of free use. They are still major sources but openly licensed content has, arguably, become more important.

One can trace the origins of open content licensing to the ideas of free software and open source. Starting in the 1980s software developers were the first to experiment with global digital markets. Certain developers in universities and activists like Richard Stallman decided to write license agreements that best utilize the new distribution channel. Thus, licenses like GNU General Public License were born and introduced concepts like copyleft. In the late 1990s, after the launch of the Word Wide Web the Internet became a distribution channel for all kind of content from text to music and pictures. Soon authors started to experiment with open content licenses.

The number of open content licenses is today high and new licenses continue to appear. Perhaps the first truly popular license was GNU Free Documentation License (GFDL) introduced by Richard Stallman's Free Software Foundation. Today, the clearly leading licensing project is Creative Commons (CC). Launched in 2001, the project offers to creators a number of different licensing options. It must be noted that CC is not a single license but a project, which has developed a set of different open content licenses that suit different needs. This chapter will focus on commenting the most popular open content licenses such as GFDL and CC-licenses, and their application.

That said, copyright was just one of the legal issues discussed in the previous chapter. Also criminal law that affects content, data protection and the editorial regulation of publications were covered. Community created content services can take these areas of law into account in their terms of services and privacy policies, which are briefly covered at the end of this chapter.

3.2   CREATIVE COMMONS LICENSES

Figure 4.

Commons Deed – an explanation of key license terms.

3.2.1 How the licensing service works

It is difficult to estimate the popularity of different open content licenses because of the short time they have been used. It seems however clear, however, that the most popular licensing initiative so far has been Creative Commons (CC). CC project was started in 2001 as an initiative to standardize more liberal license terms in content. Major United States universities have since started to advocate CC with Stanford University's law professor Lawrence Lessig in the highlight.

While Creative Commons shares much with open source and free software licensing, there are certain differences. For instance, software authors themselves have written many popular free software and open source licenses. Open source licenses have actually codified the existing sharing culture of computer programmers. To compare, Creative Commons had in the beginning a rather strict top-down approach. The licenses were originally prepared and marketed with an entity specifically founded for that purpose. Only afterwards the process of new license development became more open and democratic. The top-down approach has however potentially affected license interpretation: there does not as of yet exist such community norms as with open source licenses. It is also interesting to note that some CC-licenses go explicitly against the Open Source Definition restricting for example commercial use of the works.

In practice, Creative Commons works as an Internet service for the creation of copyright licenses in content. Users make a few choices and can then view suitable licenses. Licenses have three representations: (1) short explanation of what the license means ("commons deed"), (2) detailed legal license text ("legal code"), and (3) technical rights description. Published works are then linked to the selected license located at CC website.

Compared to a legal analysis of the licenses, it is almost trivial to take the licenses into use. CC website asks users to answer a few yes-no type question after which a suitable licenses, or a few options, are shown on the screen. Licensor has to attach selected license to the work as a hyperlink. After successfully attaching the license the website where the work is available will have a little logo stating: "CC-licensed. Some rights reserved." Clicking it links to the actual license text at the Creative Commons website.

3.2.2 License versions and incompatibility problem

There is no single "Creative Commons" license available. In fact, there are already hundreds of CC-licenses in use and the number is growing. CC-licenses are versioned through version numbers (1.0, 2.0, 2.5), languages (iCommons), and specific clauses.

From a technical perspective, CC rights description system can be used to attach almost any kind of licenses to any work distributed on the Internet. For example, the most popular free software licenses GNU GPL and LGPL are available from Creative Commons as "CC-GPL" and "CC-LGPL" branches. Further, short "Public Domain" dedication addresses a shorter expiration for copyright: a work under CC-PD would expire immediately (not including moral rights, which are non-transferable including transfer to the public).

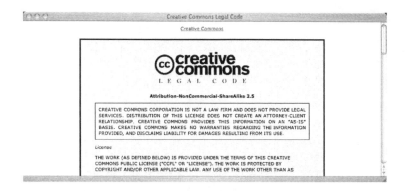

Figure 5. Legal Code – the beginning of the actual legal license text.

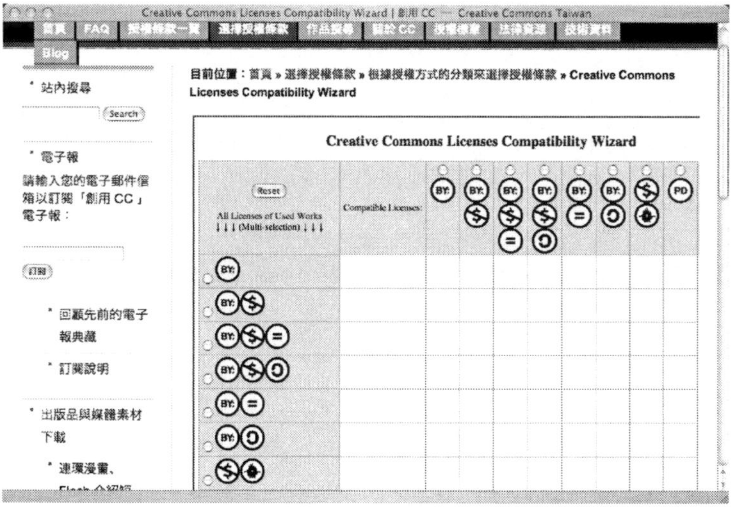

Figure 6. Creative Commons Taiwan provides a licensing wizard that helps with the relicensing of works.

In the following, this book focuses on the general CC content licenses and their specific terms. First 1.0 versions of the general CC-licenses were released in December 2002 and new "updated" 2.0 versions in May 2004. Currently the version number is 2.5 and 3.0 will be introduced in early 2007. The commentary is mainly based on the general versions 2.5 unless otherwise noted.

The general English versions are worded mainly US copyright law in mind. CC-licenses have also been translated to different languages and adapted to different jurisdictions. Creative Commons is the first major open licensing initiative, which aims at license internationalization. An assumption for internationalization is that an English language license text may not be valid outside the United States. The substantive implication of internationalization is that different language versions (iCommons) are interchangeable:

" *You may distribute, publicly display, publicly perform, or publicly digitally perform a Derivative Work only under the terms of this License, a later version of this License with the same License Elements as this License, or a Creative Commons iCommons license that contains the same License Elements as this License*

It is worth to compare the adaptations that have been produced to date and find out possible inconsistencies. Indeed, the differences seem to be significant. Obviously, the Creative Commons project has given substantial freedom to each national internationalization team. Many, but not all, try to convert the license into a contract. Some translations include notorious terminological changes (instead of distribution they may speak of making publicly available) and so on. In many cases, the definitions are taken from national copyright laws. In most adaptations, fair use is edited to match the European copyright laws, which typically include a closed list of "exceptions" to the exclusive rights. An explicit reference to database right is added on some, but not all adaptations. Only few licenses take the issue of moral rights explicitly into consideration.

Obviously, internationalization through translation and legal adaptation has the benefit of understandable licenses but it also makes them legally valid in more jurisdictions. However, the approach has also clear drawbacks. As a practical matter, the usability and interoperability of licenses may suffer because users have to deal with a number of different license versions in different languages with different terminology. There may be also possibilities to "forum shopping" inside an internationalized open content licensing project – as in the real world.

In general, the huge number of different CC-licenses imply an incompatibility problem: in many cases content under one CC-license can not be combined, re-licensed, mixed or mashed up with content under another CC-license to create a derivative or modified work. As the license says:

"   You may not offer or impose any terms on the Derivative Works that alter or restrict the terms of this License or the recipients' exercise of the rights granted hereunder.

Finally, it is always possible to make private adaptations of CC-licenses. Own adaptations should never be made to the license text itself. The modification of well-known license templates goes against the very idea of mass-market licenses and increases incompatibility problems. Further, such own changes may be invalid and they may violate the CC-trademark. Hence, if an author cannot commit to CC-license terms as they stand, the best way to amend them is to write for example additional terms on a separate webpage.

Currently own clarifications or interpretations of the license text are not possible but this may change in the upcoming version 3.0:

" *This License constitutes the entire agreement between the parties with respect to the Work licensed here. There are no understandings, agreements or representations with respect to the Work not specified here. Licensor shall not be bound by any additional provisions that may appear in any communication from You. This License may not be modified without the mutual written agreement of the Licensor and You.*

3.2.3 License grant mechanism

CC-licenses state a rather typical method for license acceptance:

" *BY EXERCISING ANY RIGHTS TO THE WORK PROVIDED HERE, YOU ACCEPT AND AGREE TO BE BOUND BY THE TERMS OF THIS LICENSE. THE LICENSOR GRANTS YOU THE RIGHTS CONTAINED HERE IN CONSIDERATION OF YOUR ACCEPTANCE OF SUCH TERMS AND CONDITIONS.*

The idea is that one is not able to copy, distribute or modify the work unless there is clear permission from the author. One gets such permission by accepting the license. It is then subject to legal debate what kind of "acceptance" procedure is needed for the license to become valid. In most countries, also non-explicit acceptance of contracts is valid. A practical justification for this is that without acceptance one would not be authorized to use the work for many purposes.

If one distributes the work further, other users will also get a similar license directly from the author. CC thus builds on the concept of direct licensing from a single author to all users. This is expressed in the license text through the following terms:

" *You may not sublicense the Work.*

" *Each time You distribute or publicly digitally perform the Work or a Collective Work, the Licensor offers to the recipient a license to the Work on the same terms and conditions as the license granted to You under this License.*

3.2.4 Common terms

(1) Since version 2.0, all CC-licenses require attribution. As noted, attribution belongs to moral rights. However, US copyright law has implemented moral rights only partially and thus it is necessary to have a separate contract clause for that. It goes as follows:

" ... *You must keep intact all copyright notices for the Work and provide, reasonable to the medium or means You are utilizing: (i) the name of the Original Author (or pseudonym, if applicable) if supplied, and/or (ii) if the Original Author and/or Licensor designate another party or parties (e.g. a sponsor institute, publishing entity, journal) for attribution in Licensor's copyright notice, terms of service or by other reasonable means, the name of such party or parties; the title of the Work if supplied; to the extent reasonably practicable, the Uniform Resource Identifier, if any, that Licensor specifies to be associated with the Work, unless such URI does not refer to the copyright notice or licensing information for the Work; and in the case of a Derivative Work, a credit identifying the use of the Work in the Derivative Work (e.g., "French translation of the Work by Original Author," or "Screenplay based on original Work by Original Author").*

Further, the common terms of CC-licenses state that attribution must be removed from collective and derivative works if so requested.

(**2**) All CC-licenses include free copying and publication rights. Anyone can thus make verbatim copies of CC-licensed content and distribute them on the Internet. As an important limitation, the copying right does not apply to any modifications, translations or derivative works.

(**3**) All CC-licenses state that the usage rights of CC-licensed content cannot be further restricted through the use of DRM systems:

" *You may not distribute, publicly display, publicly perform, or publicly digitally perform the Work with any technological measures that control access or use of the Work in a manner inconsistent with the terms of this License Agreement.*

The DRM clause also applies to derivative works. However, it does not apply to a collective work such as a book, which includes a CC-licensed picture.

(**4**) The coverage of all rights defined in CC-licenses is rather wide including also changes in copyright law:

" *The above rights may be exercised in all media and formats whether now known or hereafter devised.*

It is subject to legal debate whether far-reaching clauses like the above are valid against authors who were unaware of the future exploitation possibilities not even invented at the time of first distribution.

3.2.5 Optional license terms

(1) CC-licensors can specifically disallow modifications or derivative works ("no derivatives"). The restriction does not apply to collective works. Additionally, it does not apply to minor modifications that are required to simply use the work in its intended purpose:

" *The above rights include the right to make such modifications as are technically necessary to exercise the rights in other media and formats.*

(2) CC-licensors can also specifically attach a copyleft-obligation to the license ("share alike"). This means that all modifications, translations or derivative works must be distributed with the same CC-license as the original work. It is worth noting that the copyleft obligation does not reach to collective works:

" *You may distribute, publicly display, publicly perform, or publicly digitally perform a Derivative Work only under the terms of this License, a later version of this License with the same License Elements as this License, or a Creative Commons iCommons license that contains the same License Elements as this License.*

Case study:

LICENSES WITHOUT ATTRIBUTION

DESCRIPTION: First 1.0 versions of general CC-licenses did not require attribution although only a minimal number of CC-licensors chose to skip that requirement. That said, one can find CC-licensed content on the Internet licensed without the attribution requirement.

Assume a service provider takes the content requiring no attribution into use as such and makes necessary references to the licenses. After some time, one could have created a good reputation by providing the content but the real authors would have remained unknown. Can the authors still require attribution? How could the service provider have made it sure than no one can start a competing service with the same content?

PROBLEMS AND ADVICE: Since copyright laws do not in general allow waivers on moral rights, it is possible that the authors indeed later successfully demand to be called as the authors of those works. Another thing is that most probably their possible claims for damages would be unsuccessful.

Because all CC-licenses since 1.0 have allowed free verbatim copying and distribution, it is difficult to restrict competing services based on CC-licenses alone. Perhaps only the optional CC-clause – discussed later –, which restricts commercial use, could be used to limit competing services.

(3) CC-licensors can also specifically restrict the commercial use of the work. In fact, nearly 70 percent of the c. 150 million CC-licensed works available today are licensed with terms that include the non-commercial element.

The interpretation of "commercial" is however nothing but clear. The actual license text only states:

> "You may not exercise any of the rights granted to You ... in any manner that is primarily intended for or directed toward commercial advantage or private monetary compensation."

The only additional information, which is given about the nature of the clause, clarifies its relation to file sharing services:

> "The exchange of the Work for other copyrighted works by means of digital file-sharing or otherwise shall not be considered to be intended for or directed toward commercial advantage or private monetary compensation, provided there is no payment of any monetary compensation in connection with the exchange of copyrighted works."

The FAQ section at CC's homepage gives one example of what can be commercial use:

> "Gus publishes his photograph on his website with a Non-commercial license. Camille prints Gus' photograph. Camille is not allowed to sell the print photograph without Gus's permission."

Case study:

LICENSES THAT ALLOW COMMERCIAL USE

DESCRIPTION: Assume a journalist chooses CC-licensed pictures to visualize his article. The licenses do not have any of the optional restrictions in place. The journalist is happy: the pictures fit the story, he gets the money from the paper and there is no need to pay for the pictures. A secretary adds the names of the photographers to the story. Was there anything wrong when they did not pay to the original author and did not even contact him?

PROBLEM AND ADVICE: In short, there is no problem. The photographer has selected the license, which he wants to use. He may not be interested in monetary compensation in the first place. If he however later learns that his pictures are used for commercial advantage, he might start licensing future pictures with the non-commercial use clause. (Assuming such use can be counted commercial). To compare, requiring derivative works to be licensed with the same terms would not help since an article with an unmodified picture is counted as a collective work. The photographer might even try to re-license the pictures in question with non-commercial use clause although any copies of the work already in circulation bear the license they were first licensed with. Also, the journalist might skip his pictures after a decision to use the no-commercial use clause.

Unfortunately, there is no authoritative legal interpretation how directly related the monetary compensation has to be to the use of the work. Naturally, the sale of the content is forbidden. The interpretation is more uncertain when the content is used in a service (educational etc.), which requires a payment. For example, is a private school allowed to use non-commercial material in its classes? Is a public school allowed to ask a "copying fee" for any material, which includes the non-commercial clause?

It is common that copyright holders limit the scope of licenses to cover only certain users, geographical areas, time-frame, etc. However, copyright laws do not typically make a difference whether certain use under exclusive rights is commercial or not. The only place where such distinction is made is the remedy system where an infringement in commercial scale typically results in a stricter punishment or higher damages. In practice, the scope of the commercial use limitation is up to license interpretation.

According to general contract law, an unclear contract term will be interpreted against the party who was responsible of writing the term. Interpretation can also draw advice from the circumstances of contract negotiations and common objectives of the licensor and licensee.

However, the interpretation rules are not very useful in the case of CC-licenses. The CC-licenses are mass-market licenses that are granted to the public. Licensor does not know the future licensees or the intended uses of the licensed works. Thus the interpretation of the licensor's will is limited to parties who directly deal with the licensor at the time of the original release of the licensed works. Beyond that point making any guesses of the intention of the licensor is purely an academic exercise.

In other words, many factors hinder the interpretation of the non-commercial use clause. One is left with a few possible options to clarify the situation:

1. Clarify the commercial element by adding additional terms to the license or publishing an own interpretation in a FAQ or similar location. This might indeed help, unless the work is remixed or otherwise used to create a derivative work with another work without the clarification. Because of the incompatibility problem this option is recommend only when the author does not want anyone to create derivative works.

2. Dual license with both a CC-license and a fee-based license. The first one would be a CC-license with the non-commercial use clause and the second one a proprietary license for those commercial users, who want to use the content in a manner, which is most likely conflicting with the no commercial use clause. Dual licensing is possible as long as the rights to the content are fully owned by the licensor.

3. Change the "non-commercial use" clause to "share alike". In practice, the difference between share-alike and non-commercial is in many cases minor. Share-alike makes the monetary benefiting from the content more difficult since the downstream users are allowed to freely copy and modify the work. In other words, the commercial party may ask payments for the content, but after the first copy is out, the customers have an option to copy instead of buying. It has been proved with open source licensing that this may work remarkably well in practice. The major limitation of this approach with CC-licensing is that the "share alike" restriction does not apply to collective works. One can for example include a "share alike" licensed picture in a commercially sold book without sharing any royalties to the photographer. This is not possible with the non-commercial clause.

3.2.6 Liabilities and warranties

All CC-licenses have a rather standard-looking warranty disclaimer following the US law. CC-licenses have since version 2.0 also a standard liability disclaimer:

// *EXCEPT TO THE EXTENT REQUIRED BY APPLICABLE LAW, IN NO EVENT WILL LICENSOR BE LIABLE TO YOU ON ANY LEGAL THEORY FOR ANY SPECIAL, IN-CIDENTAL, CONSEQUENTIAL, PUNITIVE OR EXEMPLARY DAMAGES ARISING OUT OF THIS LICENSE OR THE USE OF THE WORK, EVEN IF LICENSOR HAS BEEN ADVISED OF THE POSSIBILITY OF SUCH DAMAGES.*

All the details in the disclaimers may not apply elsewhere. For example, European Union currently requires consumer contracts to use national language because consumers should understand their obligations. Also, the EU does not allow unlimited liability exceptions in consumer contracts. It is not legal to disclaim liability for actions made in bad faith. There are also minimum warranty requirements for consumer sales.

More importantly, first 1.0 versions of CC-licenses include a limited liability clause. It shifts the burden of third party infringement claims to the original licensor. The clause states:

// *By offering the Work for public release under this License, Licensor represents and warrants that, to the best of Licensor's knowledge after reasonable inquiry:*

1.   *Licensor has secured all rights in the Work necessary to grant the license rights hereunder and to permit the lawful exercise of the rights granted hereunder without You having any obligation to pay any royalties, compulsory license fees, residuals or any other payments;*

2.   *The Work does not infringe the copyright, trademark, publicity rights, common law rights or any other right of any third party or constitute defamation, invasion of privacy or other tortious injury to any third party.*

As noted, later versions of the licenses do not have such a clause but it is possible to attach one. Beneficiaries of this kind of warranty clause are for example different service providers who can take CC-licensed works into use and distribute them further with lower risk. If third party copyright has been infringed, the author may be in the end liable for the infringement.

Unfortunately, such a warranty clause is far from bullet-proof. If the author is unknown or bankrupt, the burden of third party liability will be practically on all those who are sued. This can be quite unjust especially for re-mixers and other co-authors acting in good faith. Under free licensing systems, they are not paid licensing fees for copies but they may still be held liable for copyright infringements. In other words, co-authors give the work for others to use without any compensation and, in addition, may give a limited warranty for its use – again without any compensation. In short, increased liability is one of the things that can prevent community content projects from growing.

3.2.7 Compliance and enforceability

There are not yet been many legal cases where CC-licenses would have been the issue at stake. The authors of this book are aware of just three lower court decisions discussed briefly below. Obviously, as with free software and open source licensing, compliance is largely informal. That said, one could expect that CC licenses create more problems since they are used by the general public, not computer professionals

In a Dutch lower court case decided in March 2006, the court enforced a CC-license used at Flickr that included the optional term "no commercial use". A magazine publisher had copied a picture published in Flickr without contacting the photographer to settle the obviously commercial use. The publisher also failed to give proper attribution to the photographer as required in the license. In the end, the photographer sued. The magazine publisher claimed that since the Flickr site informed visitors with the note "this photo is public" it did not have to pay anything. However, the court said that a professional publisher should be careful enough to notice that there is also a specific copyright notice saying "some rights reserved". A simple click brings forth the CC-clauses. Thus, the photographer won and a CC-license was successfully enforced.

In two contradictory cases from March and December 2006 Spanish lower courts have ruled whether bars that play only CC-licensed music are required to pay something to a collecting society. In Europe, collecting societies may ask for royalties from any users of any music, including from those artists who do not belong to the society. Thus, collecting societies have in the past been successful in negotiating annual royalties with basically all bar owners. However, in the first case the bar owner successfully proved that all the music he had played was CC-licensed and that the musicians apparently were not signed by the collecting society. The bar owner won and CC-licenses were successfully enforced. In the second case, the collecting society was able to prove that the music played included artists who had signed with the collecting society. Despite CC-licenses, the bar owner had to pay in this case royalties as if the music would have come from any source. From legal policy standpoint, the Spanish cases highlight that there is much to improve with the relationship between collecting societies and open content licensing.

3.3 OTHER RELEVANT LICENSES

Figure 7.
Wikipedia is one of the biggest community created projects.

3.3.1 GNU Free Documentation License

CC-licenses are not the only popular open content licenses. GNU Free Documentation License (GFDL) has been used extensively to license for example software manuals. The leading GFDL-licensed body of copyrighted works is today the collaborative online encyclopedia Wikipedia that has millions of articles produced by users. Three versions of the license exist so far (1.0, 1.1. and 1.2). Free Software Foundation has also released a discussion draft for version 2.0 together with a new "GNU Simpler Free Documentation License".

The license generally allows verbatim copying and distribution. However, GFDL has rather complicated rules regarding to derivate works. GFDL-licensed documents may contain specific sections, which are cannot be removed in derivate or modified works. These sections include "History", "Acknowledgements", "Dedications" and so-called invariant sections of the material, which can be for example political statements. In addition, the derivate work may not contain "Endorsements" from the original license.

Further, GFDL has special requirements if the distribution of a printed document is larger than one hundred copies:

" *If you publish or distribute Opaque copies of the Document numbering more than 100, you must either include a machine-readable Transparent copy along with each Opaque copy, or state in or with each Opaque copy a computer-network location from which the general network-using public has access to download using public-standard network protocols a complete Transparent copy of the Document, free of added material.*

A transparent copy is defined as:

" *A machine-readable copy, represented in a format whose specifica-*
tion is available to the general public, that is suitable for revising
the document straightforwardly with generic text editors or (for im-
ages composed of pixels) generic paint programs or (for drawings)
some widely available drawing editor, and that is suitable for input
to text formatters or for automatic translation to a variety of for-
mats suitable for input to text formatters.

The definition is not very clean since "widely available" is not explained. In practice it means standard and free file formats such as Open Document Format (ODF), HTML, PDF, JPG and Ogg. There is yet another problem with GFDL. It has a clause, which is aimed at preventing the use of DRM mechanisms for GFDL-licensed material:

" *You may not use technical measures to obstruct or control the read-*
ing or further copying of the copies you make or distribute.

One could say that the clause is overbroad because it applies not only to the distribution of material but also making copies for private use and secondly it effectively forbids any use of encryption. The clause is supposed to be removed from forthcoming "GNU Simpler Free Documentation License".

As a conclusion, it is generally speaking not a good idea to use GFDL under its current version unless the goal is interoperability with Wikipedia. Even in software projects GFDL is not an optimal choice since it is not compatible with copyleft licenses such as GPL. One may not be able to for example extract comments from a GPL-licensed source code and place it into a GFDL-licensed manual and vice versa.

3.3.2 Free Art License

The first popular copyleft-like open content license preceding Creative Commons was Free Art License created in 2000. The license is rather straightforward. It gives full distribution and modification rights to the users as long as the following requirements are met:

" - attach this license, in its entirety, to the copies or indicate precisely where the license can be found,
- specify to the recipient the name of the author of the originals,
- specify to the recipient where he will be able to access the originals (original and subsequent). The author of the original may, if he wishes, give you the right to broadcast/distribute the original under the same conditions as the copies.

The license does not include any special requirements for commercial use and it is also silent on DRM. Free Software Foundation also prefers the license to CC-licenses. Their website states:

"   *We recommend using the Free Art License, rather than this one [Creative Commons Attribution-Sharealike 2.0 license], so as to avoid augmenting the problem caused by the vagueness of "a Creative Commons license.*

An obvious problem with the license is its strict requirement that only works, which are licensed with it, may be combined in derivate works. Free Art License is consequently inherently incompatible with other open content licenses.

3.3.3 FreeBSD Documentation License

FreeBSD Documentation License is somewhat common in software documentation. It was originally created for the FreeBSD-operating system. The license is very simple. It has a warranty disclaimer and minor requirements that aim to preserve authors moral rights and the liability disclaimer. Copying, distribution and modification are freely allowed.

3.3.4 Open Content License

Another noteworthy license is Open Content License. It is not particularly popular but there are still community content projects, which are using it. The license's requirements are rather close to CC's Attribution-NonCommercial-ShareAlike: it does now allow commercial distribution and requires that the derivate works are licensed with the same license.

3.4 OTHER RELEVANT USAGE RULES

3.4.1 Terms of Use

As noted, community created content may be illegal based on criminal law. That does not mean that the community content service provider would be also in charge for what has been published on the service. However, the provider must comply with take-down notices and generally avoid situations where indirect criminal liability could be constructed.

Most community content service providers have detailed terms of use contracts that individual contributors must accept before they are able to submit new contributions. Their value is mainly informal: to communicate to the user what is allowed and what is not. Any breach of the terms of use means typically that the user account will be closed. The terms of use may state, for example, that:

1.   Submitting material that infringes copyright or other intellectual property rights law is not allowed.

2.   Submitting material that is illegal according to criminal law including child pornography, defamatory statements, privacy intrusion, hate speech, and explicit violence is not allowed.

Figure 8.

A snuff film of Saddam Hussein's execution taken with a cell phone spread quickly on video sharing services like YouTube. The official footage of the execution did no show the actual hanging. While these kind of videos may not be illegal in the United States where YouTube is located, many users protested the video and flagged it as "unsuitable". One needs to register and accept YouTube's Terms of Use to view it. The terms require one to affirm that one is "either more than 18 years of age, or an emancipated minor, or possess legal parental or guardian consent."

In most cases, ownership of rights into submissions remains with the submitter or whoever owns the content submitted. This makes sense for both the user and the service provider: the user keeps the control to license the work to others and the provider may avoid liability. Typically the service is given a worldwide, non-exclusive, sub-licensable and transferable right to use the copyrighted work in all possible ways according to copyright law unless limited by a certain license clause. This allows the provider flexibility in developing the service technically as well as better possibilities to sell the service business to anyone interested.

In some cases, the services also require end-users to accept the terms of use. This can be the case for example when the law defines age restrictions on sexually explicit or violent content.

3.4.2 Privacy Policies

Following EU data protection regulations, community created content services that take in user registrations must provide necessary notifications on their website. As noted, they should announce e.g. what data is being collected, how it is stored and used, where it was collected and where it can be transferred. Further, the provider must give users access to the data and allow them to correct any errors found. In practice, it has become common to state additional privacy assurances in addition to the requirements in the applicable laws.

4. Community Created Content Ecosystem

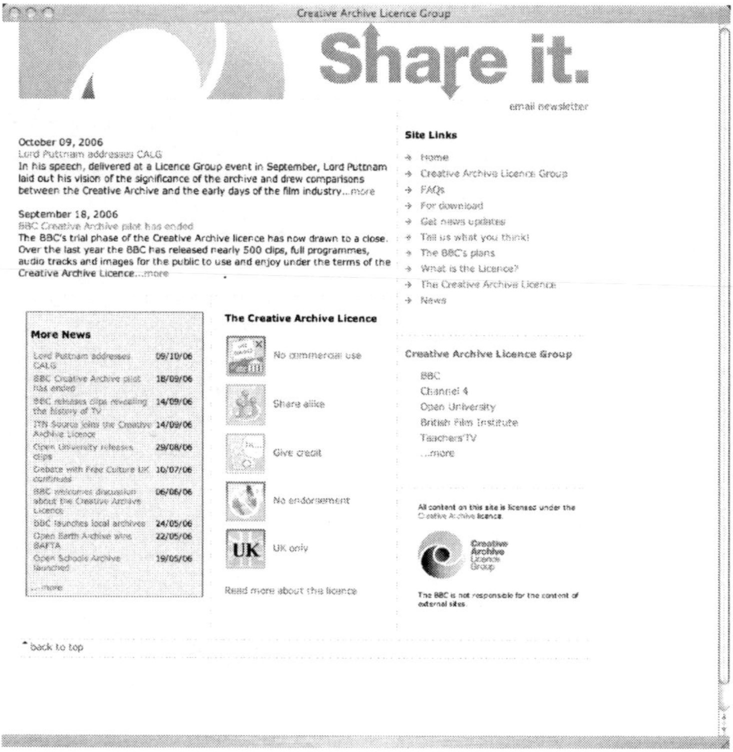

Figure 9.

BBC's creative archive uses modified CC licenses.

4.1   INTRODUCTION

Next, the book shifts focus from law to business. This section discusses different groups who want to share their work openly and license their works with open content licenses. First, this chapter examines who are the people who share their works and what are their incentives. Then the next chapter discusses what kind of business models does the open content and free distribution enable.

By examining individuals and projects, it is possible to understand, who are the people and institutions that share their works openly. In this book the users are divided to four groups. 1) Drifters 2) Public producers 3) Commonists and 4) Commercial users. The division is done by examining each group's motives of sharing.

4.2   DRIFTERS

The biggest group of users is obviously amateurs and professionals who participate in non-commercial projects. These drifters do not typically make a conscious decision to use open content licenses. Wikipedia users are typical drifters as they get carried away to projects that use open content licenses. Participating into these communities' work requires accepting the social norm of open content sharing. None of the traditional copyright incentive models explain why Wikipedia authors have helped to create one of the biggest online encyclopedias.

There are very few direct economic incentives to donate the work to Wikipedia community. Financial value may have indirect significance in cases where licenses are used to block others from tak-

Figure 10.

Hip hop band Beastie Boys share their A Capellas for remixing.

ing commercial advantage of distributed works. Moral rights and especially attribution right does not count either as a motivation because the authors of the articles are typically anonymous. Gaining respect from community plays only a limited role compared to open source programming. In the case of Wikipedia the role of copyright and law is secondary compared to the social power of the networks. Wikipedia would certainly exist even without exclusive copyright system.

4.3   PUBLIC PRODUCERS

Second group of licensors depends also on community resources. Public entities and tax funded organizations like libraries, archives and public broadcasting companies all produce content using public money. Their content is either paid by the general public or the users of the service. Providing online access to content means only a small additional expenditure compared to original production costs. Most notably BBC has opened its archives and licensed their programs with modified CC licenses for British TV-viewers. According to the FAQ at the Creative Archive website this is because: "…the member organisations who supply the content are funded with public money to serve the UK population".

While some of the information (laws and court decisions) that is produced by public bodies is public domain in most countries, a lot of publicly produced content is copyrighted ("government copyright"). Typically public content produced by public bodies is meant to be shared as widely as possible. Just recently the public sector has started to understand the relevance of copyright licenses for wide dissemination of works. For example the Finnish Information Society Council, lead by the prime minister, recommended in 2006 that public entities would adopt CC-licenses in order to encourage the flow of publicly produced information in educational sector.

4.4 COMMONISTS

The individuals in the third group have varying motives for using open content licenses. Some of them see copyright system as cultural lock that limits their creativity and human's natural need to help their neighbors. They fight the enclosure by licensing their works with open content licenses. This group can be described as Commonists. The group sees Internet as final frontier where humankind should share rather than create another area of exclusivity.

Economists have examined the incentives of open source programmers and found that many of them receive economic rewards by participating in the projects. The immediate reward comes from fixing a bug or customizing the program. Participating to successful open source project functions also as a signaling incentive. The developers get the delayed reward in a form of social capital and peer recognition and economic capital from job offers that the recognition may generate.

The incentives to share could also be limited, as it is with a sampling community. Sampling community sees that transforming pieces of works should be allowed but copying and distribution of the entire work should be up to the rights owner to decide. CC sampling licenses enable use of samples but reserve other rights. Creative Commons also helped to create CC-Mixter website that helps remixers find and share songs and samples. Sampling licenses are targeted especially to hip hop's remix culture that has been borrowing riffs and beats without asking permission for decades.

CC-Mixter enables remixers and authors to share their works and build upon other users' works. CC-Mixter has placed emphasis on letting users to see how the songs are build of different samples. Users can find other artists who have used same samples and artists can see who has used their samples.

The free sharing ideology has used "share alike" and copyleft licenses to further advance their purposes. Copyleft licenses make sure that if the changes to the work are distributed, they must use the same copyleft license terms. The free software community is using copyright licenses to preserve the freedoms they value. Preserving property in order to advance the greater good of the community resembles foundation institute. Instead of investing the property to stocks, free software movement is using its licenses to invest to new free software products which further benefit the community.

4.5   COMMERCIAL USERS

The media industry is based on a remarkable contradiction. At the same time content is more valuable when more people consume it, but the business model limits the access only to paying customers. When the physical media such as CDs and movie theatres was the prevailing way of distribution, the model worked flawlessly. Internet and new consumer technology have gradually changed the way people use content. Users do not only consume. They create, remix and share content with their peers. Most media companies have seen this trend as a threat. Others have managed to harness the potential of the user communities. The next part of this book describes business models that rely on open distribution of the content. All the models have one common denominator: the rights owner has released some control of the work as a bargain for the benefits it provides. Finding the optimal balance between access and property rights is delicate as Stanford law professor Lessig has stated: "Just because some control is good, it doesn't follow that more is better."

5. Community Content Business Models

5.1 INTRODUCTION

Open content licensors share some of the motivations with free and open source programmers. Eric Raymond wrote in his well-known essay "The Magic Cauldron" some ten years ago about open source software's indirect sale value models. He identifies models that capture the value of open source software. Open content shares most of the models but has several others. This part of the book broadens Raymond's taxonomy to open content business and examines six business models where commercial licensors use open content licenses to advance their business. These models are: 1) Loss leader 2) Open content service 3) Free the content sell the platform 4) Sell the basic product, let users enhance it 5) Outsource advertisement or advertisement distribution to users 6) Wrap open content to advertisements.

5.2 LOSS LEADER

"Loss leader" is a strategy where items are sold or given away below cost in an effort to stimulate other profitable sales. Raymond defines loss leader model as use of "open-source software to create or maintain a market position for proprietary software that generates a direct revenue stream." Most of the open content business models utilize loss leader strategy in some way or the other. Open content is used to generate demand for other content or rights that are not granted with the license. The latter strategy is called dual licensing. Releasing content may serve as advertisement. This may be especially beneficial in entertainment industry where typically half of the production costs are used to promotion. Average negative costs (production costs, studio overhead and capitalized interest) for a Motion Picture Association of America movie were 63,6 million dollars and average marketing costs of new feature films were 34,35 million dollars.

Loss leader resembles Raymond's "Sell it - Free it" business model where a company's content's product life cycle start as traditional commercial product but then it is later converted to open-content products when appropriate. Releasing part of back catalogue that is in the end of its commercial life cycle may help to create demand for other content and commercial rights. This is true especially if the content is distributed in physical form and the edition is sold out.

Loss leader strategy has been used in several music and photo services and lately with Internet movie distribution. A science fiction motion picture Star Wreck: In the Pirkinning, used teams of volunteers, digital sets, guerrilla marketing, and the Internet to produce, promote, and distribute the film to a global audience. Creators minimized the overall costs of production while producing a professional quality feature-length movie that reached over 5 million viewers within its first 6 months. Even thought the movie is distributed freely online using a Creative Commons license, it has sold thousands of copies of DVDs, and the TV broadcast rights alone have covered the production costs of the movie. A year after the initial release Universal pictures bought the distribution rights

Figure 11.
Director Timo Vuorensola holding the imperial edition of Star Wreck.

Figure 12.
Flickr's Creative Commons page.

to the special edition version of the DVD. Star Wreck has showed how readily available digital technology and fan communities can be used to reduce considerably the cost of making movies. Furthermore, the movie's success also proved that Internet distribution does not preclude financial success, but on the contrary may open international markets for amateur producers.

5.3 SELL SERVICES

Content creators need several tools to create and distribute digital content. Authoring tools, hosting services, and community websites are all part of the chain from creators to users.

Flickr photo hosting service is targeting heavy users who want to share their photos online. Professional users get unlimited storage capacity on Flickr servers for a $ 25 annual fee. Flickr's advantage to its competitors is a very active community, simple user interface and a wide range of options. Flickr provides access to its application programming interface (API) even to its competitors if they also have an open API. Open interfaces enable users to easily switch to and transfer their files to a new service. Openness enables competition but also complementary services that create value to Flickr users. Flickr enables users to set their sharing level from strict private access to generous CC-licenses. On September 2006 over 10 percent of Flickr's total of 200 million photos were licensed with CC-licenses. Users can search the photos by tags and used licenses.

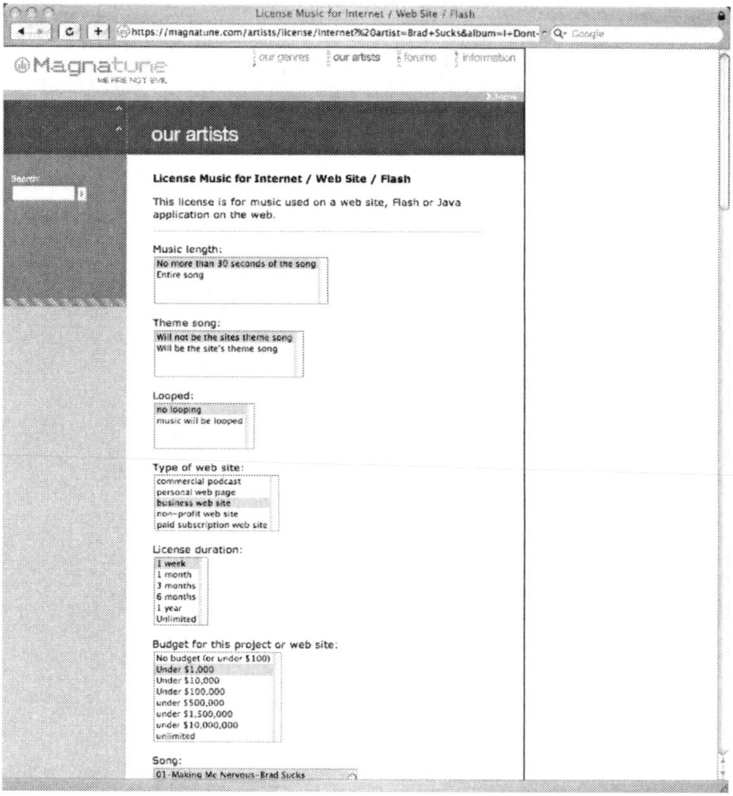

Figure **13.**

Magnatune runs an online license supermarket.

Online record label Magnatune distributes its artists' music with a non-commercial CC-license. Magnatune makes its profit by selling physical CDs, high quality audio downloads and licenses to commercial use. Buying a license is made easy. Licensees can use a website to calculate license fee and after the fee is paid the license is valid. Magnatune's music licensing contract is the same to all buyers, which removes legal fees as a built-in cost. While the model is a good example of loss leader strategy, Magnatune is also an excellent illustration of services sold to content producers. Unlike regular record companies that share small percentages of their profits, Magnatune shares 50% of the licensing, CD-sales and merchandise revenue (not profit) with artists.

Magnatune also acts as an intermediary guaranteeing that the content is licensable. Traditionally collecting societies have sold licenses to users and warranted that they represent the rights owners. Open content risk management can provide business to private warranty services that track down the rights holders and validates their licenses. The risk of accidental infringement and damages could mean that indemnity and copyright insurance services could become a part of services offered by insurance companies. Software industry has traditionally used indemnification clauses as common practice when dealing with free and open source software. Several insurance companies have already started selling special policies targeted to open source software users.

"   Newspapers will change, not die
— RUPERT MURDOCH, THE INDEPENDENT, MARCH 20, 2006

Figure **14.**

Scoopt takes advantage of the long tail phenomenon

Figure **15.**

Scoopt words helps bloggers to sell their stories.

Scoopt's slogan reflects their service's idea: "If it's good enough to print, it's good enough to pay for." Scoopt runs two services for citizen journalists: 1) Scoopt picture agency and 2) Scoopt Words blogging aggregator.

Scoopt picture agency is selling user created photos on an exclusive deal. They share the revenue 50-50 with the copyright owner. Scoopt chooses photos that it offers to media houses and sets the price for the licenses. Scoopt sells three sorts of licenses: 1) exclusive licenses for photo series of scoop images, 2) non-exclusive to different publications, and 3) stock photos. Scoop is using also Flickr to host images. Flickr users can tag their photos with "scoop"-tag. That enables Scoopt to find pictures that are owned by Scoopt users and license them even if they are not in their own picture archive.

Scoopt Words service provides a market between bloggers and commercial publishers. After free registration for Scoopt membership, bloggers can add a Scoopt Words button to their site that flags their blog post as available for sale. Newspaper and magazine editors can then click the Scoopt Words button to license blog content for commercial use. The blogger receives 75% of the sales revenue (50% for the first transaction).

Scoopt Words believes that "nothing should hinder the free exchange of content - pictures, videos, words - on the internet so long as nobody is profiting at the expense of another." This is why Scoopt Words has an interface where bloggers can add a Creative Commons Attribution-NonCommercial license to their blog alongside the Scoopt commercial badge. The Creative Commons license lets authors easily and efficiently signal to the public that their work may be freely shared, reused, and remixed by people for non-commercial purposes.

Figure 16.

Down and Out in the Magic Kingdom book cover. Original cover in the front and user created alternative covers behind it.

5.4   FREE THE CONTENT - SELL THE PLATFORM

*"   I've been giving away my books ever since my first novel came out,
and boy has it ever made me a bunch of money.*
— CORY DOCTOROW, FORBES, DECEMBER 1, 2006

Raymond's second model "widget frosting" generates business to
hardware manufacturers who distribute preinstalled open source
software with their hardware. Software is given away in order to
generate market for special hardware and services. In a way selling
books works the same way. Content alone is not generating profits.
The user interface of a book is still superior to e-paper and to lap-
tops, and people are willing to pay for it. One can call the model as
"free the content sell the platform".

Science fiction writer and activist Cory Doctorow released his
first novel "Down and out in Magic Kingdom" with CC-license.
Online version of the book helps the audience to find the author
and gives a chance to preview the book before making the pur-
chase decision. Doctorow's book was not just previewed. It was remixed, translated, podcasted and downloaded 75 000 times during
the first month of its release. The online availability and extensive
blog-marketing generated buzz and by July 2006 the hard copy had
sold three print runs and over sixty-five thousand copies.

The book was not the only platform that was sold. According
to Doctorow book sales were secondary compared to paid speaking appearances that the attention generated. Hearing Doctorow
live and owning his book are the experiences that his audience and
companies pay for.

Figure **17.**

On the right is a model that inspired Lingerie Model 10 character design.

5.5 SELL THE BASIC PRODUCT, LET USERS ENHANCE IT

This model is closely related to the previous one. Users who enhance the basic product bring added value to the original without the burden of development costs to the product manufacturer. This has been noted especially in computer games. The Sims computer game is a good example of a basic product enhanced by community created content. The Sims game enables users to modify game characters and environments.

Participating to open source software project requires at least basic coding skills. Still, the most succesful projects have thousands of developers. Open content has even more potential contributors if necessary tools are provided the with content. The Sims comes with modification tools that enable playters to create their own stories, characters, lots and objects and their website has an exchange area for sharing the player created content. Players can mix their own parts with official content and content created by the other players. For example "Lingerie model 10" -character uses eyebrows and lips that were created by other players and skin tones created by a female character designer SharpeiVampire.

Stomp is a Singaporean community news site. According to Stomp's editor Jennifer Lewis readers mostly use Stomp to "upload pictures from their mobile phones of everything that annoyed them that day, including bad parking, drivers ignoring traffic lights, seat hogs on public transport, or long queues at service windows." Stomp's approach and the use of new technology have managed to attract young people to write and submit news.

Figure 18.

Stomp is a community news website built by The Straits Times.

Stomp's mother company Straits Times (ST) interacts with Stomp users in two ways:

1. ST's editorial staff and experts answer questions that are submitted by Stomp users in "Ask the ST Anything". "English as it is broken" has proved a popular element, encouraging people to submit examples of poor English from street signs and other media. ST provides ministry of education's English language specialists who comments and explains the grammatical glitches.

2. Stories submitted to Stomp are picked up by ST frequently and printed along with Stomp logo.

By having an open discussion with its users, Stomp activates its users to generate stories that are local and personal. Lewis says that giving the credit to original author and linking back to the story "builds the credibility of the story initiator, creates interest in their peer group, helps other users identify with the ST, and generates further publicity for Stomp."

The newspaper benefits from the active Stomper community that submits pictures and stories and gains revenue from banner ads. Stomp has rules of conduct that let them revoke any user's posting rights. The expenses of running a community website are low. Content mainly comes from the users and as with any good community website the system is self-policing with Stompers reporting inappropriate posts.

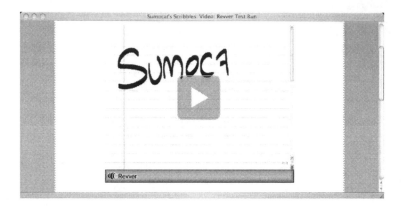

Figure **19.**

Revver videos are typically distributed through blogs.

Figure **20.**

Revver serves an ad at the end of the video.

5.6   WRAP OPEN CONTENT WITH COMMERCIALS

Revver is a video sharing service that enables rights owners to make money by sharing their films. In October 2006 it hosted over 100 000 videos. Revver differs from YouTube in three ways:

1.   Revver's video patrol reviews every video entering the Revver library for infringement, hate speech or porn.

2.   Revver shares its ad revenue 50-50 with the videos rights owner.

3.   Major part of Revver videos are not shared through Revver's website.

The key technology behind Revver is the RevTag, which is attached to videos that users upload. The RevTag tracks the videos and automatically displays a static, clickable one frame ad at the end of each video. When viewers click on it, the advertiser is charged and the advertising fee is split between the video creator and Revver.

The Revver system enables videos to be superdistributed through various channels. RevTags can be attached directly to Flash and QuickTime video files. This means that the ads are served no matter where the video file is hosted or displayed. Unlike in other video services that are serving their ads next to the video, Revver users are encouraged to share Revver videos as widely as possible. The advantage of using widely accepted video formats is that users do not have to download any additional software.

Rights owners can control what kinds of advertisements are attached to the videos. They can for example opt out tobacco or

Figure **21.**

In 2006 two amateur movie makers at Northern Maine shot a video (available at http://www.eepybird.com) of extraordinary fountains they made by dropping Mentos mints to Diet Coke bottles. The film quickly became viral and within weeks they received over six million views which generated them more than $ 35 000 in Revver ad revenue.

government ads. Because ads are dynamically delivered, rights owners' preferences take effect instantly. Revver enables rights owners to monitor where the content is viewed, how many people have watched it and how many people click the advertisements. Advertisers can buy their slots to individual films, by keywords, services and by the popularity of films. Advertisers only pay for served ads.

Revver's affiliate program persuades users to share more. An Affiliate is a user who helps to promote Revver videos. Promoting can be done through email, peer-to-peer networks, or posting the video to blogs or on social-networking web pages like MySpace. Revver affiliates earn 20% of ad revenue for the videos they help to share. The remaining revenue for each video is split 50-50 between the video creator and Revver. This is possible because the RevTag contains information not only about the video being played but also about the affiliate.

The films are distributed with Attribution-NonCommercial-NoDerivs CC-license. In addition to CC-license, copyright owners grant Revver commercial rights to serve ads and other people to host the content.

5.7 SELL THE PRODUCT, LET USERS ADVERTISE IT

Habbo Hotel is a virtual meeting place on the Internet where the gamers can create own characters and decorate a hotel room where characters can visit. Habbo Hotel is owned and developed by Sulake Inc, and it currently has 3 million monthly users worldwide.

Habbo Hotel has a devoted fan community that publishes their own fan web pages that are graphically and thematically similar to the Habbo Hotel game. Sulake encourages the gamers to create their own fan sites but keeps control over the created content by having strict terms of use for the copyrighted Habbo images and other material. For example, the fan sites that use copyrighted material must have original Habbo content that does not promote any adult, illegal, or hacking websites or websites that conflict with Sulake's interests. Also, by leveraging its copyright to the Habbo-related material, Sulake uses licensing terms that are somewhat unfamiliar to regular copyright licenses. For example, official Habbo fan sites are required to be updated at least once a month. Sulake has been also enforcing its licensing terms by forcing the closing of inappropriate fan sites.

From the fan sites point of view the strict terms of use and respective enforcing of the terms can be seen limiting the creativeness of the fans – one of the main advantages associated with community created content. Also, the creation of Habbo-related content by users is dictated by the terms of use given by Sulake. This contractual binding imposes the issue of liability to the people behind the fan sites, and in the potential case of copyright infringement the problem of responsibility among the content creators. From Sulake's perspective enforcing the terms of use and disclaimers on fan pages are critical in maintaining its brand image as a virtual world suitable for children and not allowing the dilution of its trademark by letting fans use it freely. By limiting the use of their copyrighted material Sulake is able to control the use of the content.

Internet companies are not the only ones who have noticed the power of peer advertising. Politicians have used peer-to-peer distribution long before Internet. Pamphlets and little red books were the cornerstone of communism propaganda and C-cassettes played an important role in Iran's Islamic revolution. Today Internet is a key part in the battle for voters. Harnessing political activists online means wider visibility and more campaign contributions.

Some individuals are more influential than others in convincing their friends and neighbors on what to buy and whom to vote. A report by the Institute of Politics, Democracy, & the Internet found that 69% of politically active Internet users can be considered influential. Other researchers say that only a minority of the whole population are influential. Politically active Internet users are also significantly more likely to donate money to candidates. For example in the 2004 US presidential campaign, almost every other politically active Internet user donated to a candidate or political party, compared to just 10% of the general public.

MoveOn.org has used Internet to "bring real Americans into the political process". The movement has over 3 million members who contributed 9 million dollars to "progressive candidates" and campaigns. During the 2004 US presidential elections MoveOn tried to buy a Super bowl advertisement spot for the winner of bushin30seconds contest. CBS refused to sell the spot claiming that the ad was too controversial to be broadcasted.

Licensing the content with open content licenses has two major PR-benefits. First, the content has an unlimited audience potential. Second, the reliability of the "raw" content from a blog or a video sharing service can be higher compared to packaged content from traditional organizations. Users may eventually trust on community content more than content from other sources.

Case study:

HOCKEY MEDIA PRODUCTION

DESCRIPTION: Hockey Media is an imaginary company that sells videos that are combined from hockey fans own home videos and camera phone shots from the hockey arenas. Hockey Media already has a web service where fans are discussing hockey issues on discussion forums and sharing their memories from games. Hockey Media wants to provide tools for the users to combine content that is produced by other members into multimedia. Tools would enable users to take material that is produced by someone else in the community or by professional producers and combine it to their personal media. Website enables users to create videos and photo collages that can be used for example in blogs.

Hockey Media wants to sell content that is produced by the community to TV after their producer team has edited the material into suitable form. Hockey Media also wants to use the content in their merchandise. It is planning to sell fans t-shirts and mouse pads that have fan's own pictures printed on.

Hockey Media has invested a lot of money to the community site and wants to secure that investment. The biggest fear is that competing sites would benefit from the openness that the site provides.

ADVICE: The most user friendly way to keep users on Hockey Media service is to provide superior service. This includes flawless user interface and fair terms of use.

From technical standpoint the service can try to protect itself against competition by attaching unique watermarks to the content. This way users can identify the source and link better with Hockey Media. Technology and formats can also enable user and content "lock in". For example, flash video may be harder to export from the service than avi-video clips.

Dual licensing – While the content might be available to be used only for non-commercial use, Hockey Media needs to get a license that permits them to also use it for commercial use. This permission could be easily granted when users join the community and accept the use agreement. After receiving the commercial license Hockey Media would have an advantage over its competitors who can only use the content on Hockey Media site with the same terms as the rest of the community.

Using user-generated content in advertising can go awry. In March 2006 General Motors launched a do-it-yourself ad contest to promote the Chevy Tahoe SUV. The contest challenged people to make their personal SUV commercial by combining GM provided video clips and sound tracks with their own texts. Many of the entrants used the ads to criticize the company and its products. The spots showed the car, against a backdrop of rugged glaciers and melting snow while messages appeared onscreen accusing GM of contributing to global warming. According to GM, users submitted more than 21 000 ads. While more than 80 percent of the commercials depict the Tahoe in a favorable light, the negative ads got the biggest coverage in the media backfiring GM's viral marketing effort. Many of the negative ads kept living long after the competition at video sharing services like YouTube.

Figure 22.

Video contest on Bushin30seconds website.

Figure 23.

Chevy Tahoe commercials on YouTube.org.

5.8 CONCLUDING REMARKS

The motivations to license content with open content licenses vary. Open content may serve ideological ends, public sector's goals, or it can give advantages in the marketing and distribution of digital goods. Choosing suitable licenses and a business model help right owners to keep control of the financially important use of the content.

Having reviewed business models that support open content development, one can try to answer the question: when does open content make economic sense? Rights holders can choose to license their works with open content license because the market a) has dried, b) it has never existed c) it is somewhere else than in limiting access and wide distribution helps to reach it, or d) right holders want to shift development and marketing costs to users. Open content licenses enable rights owners to stay in control compared to the option of releasing the works into public domain. Inevitability licensor loses some control of the work and this is why the model does not suit a considerable part of the current right owners. As Chevy's ad campaign shows the lack of control may lead to unwanted outcomes. These risks should be taken into account when making licensing choices. Limiting the use of the content to non-pejorative uses may help to protect the goodwill value of the company as the case of Habbo Hotel shows.

The key characteristic of a succesful open content system is the ease of use. When direct reward is lacking and indirect reward may be limited, the contributors may be turned off by complex systems. Creating a successful open content service requires interesting content that can be easily modified. This means that in addition to providing content, the service has to have a good user interface and it may have to provide tools for users to create and remix the content.

6. Policy Issues

6.1   INTRODUCTION

This chapter is dedicated to more "environmental" questions related to community content production. The demands to change the current copyright policy and usage practices have gained much popularity recently. The authors of this book believe that much of the detailed critique is based on good reasons – the current system is simply inefficient. With relatively minor steps the copyright environment could be improved to support the creation of new and innovative services. One of the biggest keys in the puzzle is the role of the copyright collective societies, which has to be reviewed in the light of the recent development. The chapter ends by discussing some problems inside the licensing projects. The risk of license incompatibility is one of the major challenges for the growth of community content services and it has to be solved even if that means bruising some egos of the current opinion leaders.

6.2   COPYRIGHT POLICY

Next this book discusses four concrete legislative steps, which could advance the opportunities for user-based content creation. The first two proposals – limiting the sanctions for non-wilful infringement and clarifying the limits of derivate use – aim to (obviously) reduce the legal risks associated to publishing material from the users. The last two proposals would establish new sources for getting legal material for user-based content creation.

6.2.1 Limitations to liability rules

As described earlier, copyright liability is currently based on a strict liability doctrine: even non-willful infringers have have to pay. Moreover, the fight against piracy has led to increasingly harsh additional criminal penalties for copyright violations. For example, in Finland the requirement of commercial purpose was removed from the definition of "copyright crime" in the beginning of 2006.

Liability issues have been harmonized to some extent through the enforcement directive and may be further harmonized if the new enforcement directive is finally accepted. The combined effect of these directives leaves little space for national legislature. Furthermore, the Convention on Cybercrime requires that there is a possibility for direct criminal sanctions (fines) for corporations.

From business perspective, extensive liabilities may create obstacles for new business models. Especially indirect liability (aiding, abetting and inciting) cover a wide range of actions so that reasonable caution remains a necessary requirement for any community content service provider. To be sure, the actual risk may not be as high as the statutes suggest because monitoring costs are so high.

The liability rules could be in any case clarified by separating "classical commercial piracy" from new innovative services, which stretch the borders of acceptable uses of copyrighted services. The latter class could be excluded from criminal sanctions and also the damages calculation could be limited to actual proven damages from the right holders. Furthermore, there could be a statutory limit on how much additional litigation costs could be included to the damages. – Another issue is that this kind of change in law does not seem realistic in the near future.

6.2.2 Clarification of derivate works

For community content creation, the rules for using existing works are in central place regarding the limits of creativity. Normal licensing fees can be prohibitively expensive for non-commercial purposes and more serious licensing negotiations may be too expensive for many small and medium sized companies. It is often not even possible to get a license for a certain use.

Copyright law is supposed to balance the situation with user rights. However, the EU copyright directive recognizes only two general user rights, which allow derivative use of works without permission from the right holder. The first one is the right to make quotations, which has further detailed requirements:

§   *d) quotations for purposes such as criticism or review, provided that they relate to a work or other subject-matter which has already been lawfully made available to the public, that, unless this turns out to be impossible, the source, including the author's name, is indicated, and that their use is in accordance with fair practice, and to the extent required by the specific purpose;*

The second right is for uses, which somehow alter the work itself in a critical way:

§   *(k) use for the purpose of caricature, parody or pastiche;*

Unfortunately, due to the extensive harmonization there is very little chance that more user rights would be added in the near future. Thus, the only feasible way to extend user rights is legal interpretation. For example, by changing what is considered to be a significant (in copyright sense) part of the work, the level of legal re-use could be adjusted because it is legal to use non-significant (or original) parts of the copyrighted material.

An illustrating example is perhaps the use of samples in music. Currently there are certain right holders that insist that any use of a sample requires a license. These "sample trolls" either raise significantly the cost of making music or alternatively limit drastically the available sources for samples. The problem was also recognized in the recently published "Gowers Review of Intellectual Property" by the UK government. The study calls for significant change on how transformative works are defined under current EU legislation:

"   *At present it would not be possible to create a copyright exception for transformative use … as it is not one of the exceptions set out as permitted in the Information Society Directive. However, the Review recommends that the Government seeks to amend the Directive to permit an exception along such lines to be adopted in the UK.*

Recommendation 11: Propose that Directive 2001/29/EC be amended to allow for an exception for creative, transformative or derivative works, within the parameters of the Berne Three-Step Test.

As noted, any changes in the directive are not likely to happen in the near future. An intermediate solution is to thus to change the interpretation practice. For example in the United States document film produces have created internal code of conduct "Best Practices in Fair Use", which describes acts that should be considered to be normal (non-licensed) use of existing works. Accordingly, documentary filmmakers must choose whether or not to rely on fair use when their projects involve the use of copyrighted material. The code of conduct is organized around four classes of situations that they confront regularly in practice. (These four classes do not exhaust all the likely situations where fair use might apply; they reflect the most common kinds of situations that documentarians identified at this point.) In each case, a general principle about the applicability of fair use is asserted, followed by qualifications that may affect individual cases.

These kinds of documents are naturally not strictly legally binding but never the less form a strong guidance for courts on what should be permissible behaviour. As long as Creative Commons does not provide mediation services and create its own "case law", creating similar code of conducts for different open content services would therefore present one realistic way to limit the legal liabilities without restricting the creative force.

6.2.3 Orphan works

Due to the long duration of copyright and the lack of formal registration, the ownership of a certain work is often very hard or even
impossible to establish reliably. As a consequence a great number
of copyrighted works is currently not utilized. The United States
Library of Congress describes the problem in the following way:

*"   A situation often described is one where a creator seeks to incor-
porate an older work into a new work (e.g., old photos, footage or
recordings) and is willing to seek permission, but is not able to
identify or locate the copyright owner(s) in order to seek permission. While in such circumstances the user might be reasonably
confident that the risk of an infringement claim against this use is
unlikely, under the current system the copyright in the work is still
valid and enforceable, and the risk cannot be completely eliminated.
Moreover, even where the user only copies portions of the work in
a manner that would not likely be deemed infringing under the
doctrine of fair use, it is asserted by some that the fair use defense
is often too unpredictable as a general matter to remove the uncer-
tainty in the user's mind.*

Some have claimed that many potential users of "orphan works",
namely individuals and small entities, may not have access to legal
advice. They cannot fully assess the risk themselves. Moreover, even
if they are able to determine that there is little or no risk of losing a
lawsuit, they may not be able to take the risk of having to bear the cost
of defending themselves.

This problem has to be solved on statutory level. Currently there is a real chance that the United States will enact legislation that addresses the problem. If that happens, it creates significant political pressure for European Union to follow the example.

The authors of this book believe that the optimal solution would be a system that requires registration of works after a certain period (5-20 years) from the publication if the right holder still insists for retaining full commercial control of the work. An intermediate solution might include for example a way to put money on an account for possible copyright claims and a procedure to demand in public the right holder(s) of a work to identify themselves.

The aforementioned Gowers Review has three concrete suggestions for the issue of orphan works that are universally applicable:

1. Propose a provision for orphan works to the European Commission, amending Directive 2001/29/EC.

2. The Patent Office should issue clear guidance on the parameters of a 'reasonable search' for orphan works, in consultation with rights holders, collecting societies, rights owners and archives, when an orphan works exception comes into being.

3. The Patent Office should establish a voluntary register of copyright, either on its own or through partnerships with database holders, by 2008.

6.2.4 Government copyright

It was already noted that governments create significant amounts of copyrighted works and their interest should typically be to distribute them as widely as possible. The first major debated issue is whether the government should have copyright in the first place. For example, in United States the works prepared for the government are not entitled to copyright protection:

§   *§ 105. Subject matter of copyright:*
United States Government works

Copyright protection under this title is not available for any work of the United States Government, but the United States Government is not precluded from receiving and holding copyrights transferred to it by assignment, bequest, or otherwise.

In Europe only the United Kingdom has currently special rules for governmental works called "Crown Copyright". The rules allow relative free use of works if certain steps (e.g. source is mentioned) are met.

The authors of this book believe it is difficult to argue why works prepared with tax payers' money should be entitled to copyright. The economic incentive for creation does not arise from licensing fees and also the second traditional reason for copyright – securing the publication of works – can be solved otherwise.

Second major issue is governmental re-use. Governments are producing significant amounts of material, which has potential to be further commercialized. A typical example is weather data, which has a wide range of possible uses beyond normal weather forecasts sent in TV and radio. The big question is, how this material should be licensed. In the United States the government requires only a certain low fee for such material and does not set any detailed usage restrictions. In Europe, the Commission's original position to the Proposal for a Directive of the European Parliament and of the Council on the re-use and commercial exploitation of public sector documents suggested following the US policy. Unfortunately the governmental institutions, which get their income from the licensing fees, managed to change the directive in this regard. It seems that there is currently not enough political will to change the regime to a US-style cost-only approach.

6.3 OPEN CONTENT AND COLLECTING SOCIETIES

Open content licensing and copyright collectives in Europe have two major problems. First, if an author wishes to use the services of collecting societies, he must typically assign the collecting society necessary exclusive rights to the work. This means that the author can no longer license the work, or any version of it, on the Internet with open content or any other terms that conflict with the policies of the collecting society in question. Second, collecting societies have in general the right to represent also those authors, which are not signed with the society. This means that a user may be obliged to pay royalties to the society even though the author has chose to use an open content license.

The first problem can be illustrated with the policy of the Finn-ish local copyright collecting society for performing artists and composers (Teosto). The society does not charge anything from authors who preview their own works at their own homepages. However, the previews must be free of charge, non-commercial and non-published. In addition, the author must not allow copy-ing or redistribution of the previews. In effect, a member of Teosto cannot use CC-licenses. The second problem was already high-lighted in the Spanish court cases discussed in the section on en-forceability. In effect, it may not be possible for example to play CC-licensed content in bars without paying royalties to a collect-ing society in Europe.

Obviously, the strong and sometimes even legally backed role of copyright collecting societies as the protectors of authors' interests has been quite easy to defend in the past. If transaction costs have been too high for individual authors to both license and collect li-censing fees themselves, it has been definitely rational to rely on a collectively administered system.

However, it is more difficult to argue why a collecting society should make the Internet as a marketing and distributing medium so diffi-cult to use. Of course, it is challenging to argue why free distribution should be allowed in side with commercial licensing. One option is to make a difference between popular and less popular works: in the end the vast majority of works whose rights are managed by collecting societies and publishers have a very short, if any, commercial lifespan. Unless it is highly probable that commercial licensing for fee would make a strong business case for a given work, the default action should be to license it always for free independent of commercial aspirations.

This brings us to the practical question of how could one apply more liberal licenses such as Creative Commons to already published works. The first option would be for collecting societies to change their policies. Such a policy change would require extensive economic research of the benefits and costs of allowing member to use CC-licensing. Reducing collecting societies' role to bare license collection would eliminate some of the costs related to interpretation and enforcement of the licenses. The cost of licensing would be on licensee and the enforcement on the licensor.

Some experts see that given today's technology the creation of a "universal" copyright registry, in exchange for incremental benefits to authors, would be highly attractive. The burden on authors is minor in exchange for what is likely to be a very substantial benefit to those who seek to republish that author's work. The registry could enable licensees to check that the content is legally licensed by verifying right owner's permissions. Users would eventually get used to legal metadata and learn to respect copyrights. A verification server could also include pricing information of the commercial rights, peer evaluation of the music, links to similar music and an ecommerce site where commercial rights and fan products would be for sale. A registry would dramatically reduce the transactions costs of licensing. It would also serve users who could verify that content is legally distributed and thus reduce risk of infringement.

A second option would be to force reforms on collecting societies. The European Commission has lately shown interest of dismantling all barriers to competition for copyright societies. Unfortunately the Commissions' decisions have not had the desired effect on competition and legislation seems inevitable.

The third option would be to develop copyright law in a way that gives the author the ability to get his copyright back in limited cases for re-licensing under reasonable circumstances. Some countries have enacted laws on copyright contracts with the intention of balancing the negotiation power of individual authors with publishers. Under certain conditions it is even possible for an author to terminate the publishing contract and republish the work under new terms.

The collecting societies as well as the open content licenses serve the public by lowering transaction costs. Finding a way to combine the two institutions could mean all the artists receiving payments for the use of their works and at the same time consumer would have more culture available on creators' terms. In order to reach the goal both institutions must make changes. Creative Commons must clarify its licenses and modify them to fit to the automatic licensing scheme of the collecting societies'. The collecting societies on their behalf have to open their paternalistic administration systems to reflect the changed motivations of rights owners and the new business models they are using.

6.4   INTERPLAY BETWEEN DIFFERENT LICENSING PROJECTS

As noted, one of the most crucial problems with open content licensing is the incompatibility problem. It could be perhaps best tackled through better mutual coordination with different licensing initiatives.

6.4.1 Free Software Foundation and Creative Commons

Free Software Foundation (FSF) is arguably the most important actor in the free software as well as open source community. Its leader Richard Stallman used to support Creative Commons but he has since changed his position:

" *I used to support Creative Commons, but then it adopted some additional licenses which do not give everyone that minimum freedom, and now I can no longer endorse it as an activity...Since people tend to treat Creative Commons as a unit, disregarding the details like which one of their licenses is being used, it is not feasible to support just part of Creative Commons--so I can't support it at all now. I asked the leaders of Creative Commons privately to change their policies, but they declined, so we had to part ways.*

In other words, Stallman and FSF could support the more permissive CC-licenses but since people do not see the difference between them and more restrictive licenses, they are forced to draw their support altogether to keep their message clear. FSF suggest that people should use instead Free Art License (for artistic works) or GNU Free Documentation License for textbooks and similar fact-oriented works. GNU Free Documentation License and GPL are incompatible with CC-licenses.

The situation is obviously not optimal. There is a real risk that the pool of open content will be fragmented to incompatible sections. Moreover, considering the dominant role GPL (and LGPL) in open source software, the split between CC and FSF realms could hamper seriously the possibilities to create interactive content based on open source and open content. The upcoming version 3 of GPL may ease the situation since it will include more relaxed rules on interoperability and thus allow wider mixing of material.

On practical level, the situation can be mitigated by using dual licensing strategies. Of course, this solution does not work in all cases i.e. some business models do not work with fully "free" licenses.

6.4.2 Debian and Creative Commons

Another important free software community, the Debian Project, has been critical towards Creative Commons. The Debian Free Software Guidelines has two requirements, on derivative works and the non-discrimination of for example commercial uses, which are in conflict of the most restrictive CC-license clauses. It can be noted that Debian also considers GNU Free Documentation License to be non-free if it includes a so-called "invariant" section.

The upcoming version 3.0 CC-licenses may cause additional problems. Depending of the exact wording, the section about DRM may be against Debian's Giudelines. However, the negotiations to avoid further problems are taking place and it is possible that a mutually acceptable compromise will be found on the question.

7. Conclusions

This book has presented an overview of the complex legal, business and policy issues in community created content. First, the book briefly went through the major doctrines in copyright law as well other laws regulating community created content services. Anyone wishing to start a new service should have a general understanding of the most relevant laws that affect community created content services. Then, the book turned to open content licensing. Creative Commons is a leading but somewhat controversial project. However, Creative Commons copyright licenses are tested and can be recommended for most community content services – with the general reservations that apply to all licensing decisions.

From law the book switched to business. It is subject to wild guesses what is the real business impact of community created content in the long term. In fact, the impact is already difficult to measure as the boundaries between community content and traditionally produced content blur. One scenario is that what one can today label as "community created content" will be just "content" in the future. The example of YouTube shows that community created content services may be just one acquisition away from major media companies. Something similar has happened to open source software. On the other hand, there remain also community-based projects such as Wikipedia, which cannot be sold. This reminds of the free software ideology, which stresses societal impact over business impact.

Finally, the book discussed the details of actual policy issues in community created content. Copyright has been the hot potato of Internet policy as long as the Internet has existed. It is also in the heart of community created content. As many other books before, this book went through a set of carefully though proposals to change copyright doctrines to reflect better the Internet reality. While the suggestions may not be implemented any time soon they should anyhow create a basis for further discussion. The book also suggested some intermediate alternatives for community content risk management. For example, best practice documentation for different aspects of copyright management may work as a shield against negligence-claims. Another major issue is the interplay between different licensing projects. No one needs another licensing project to produce another set of incompatible licenses.

Main conclusions of this book can be summarized as follows:

1.   Like other Internet services, also community created content services are subject to a number of laws. Laws are national but the services are typically open to anyone coming from any jurisdiction. Thus, it makes sense for example to use copyright licenses that are not tied to any specific national law and follow the strict privacy laws in Europe even if the service is not based in Europe.

2.   Notice-and-takedown procedures are an effective way for community content service providers to shield against copyright infringement claims in the EU and the United States. In Europe, the shield extends beyond copyright as well. However, service providers have to be careful in following the procedures defined in law.

3. Creative Commons licenses are clearly the most popular of all open content licenses and their validity has been tested before the court of law. However, one must make difficult choice on the specific optional terms before using them. For a community content service provider, it often makes sense to a) get additional rights required for the service in an user agreement and b) let the users choose from a variety of options and c) make it clear that the ownership of rights remains with the users.

4. Community created content can be the start of a new business. There are a number of examples out there ranging from YouTube to Wikipedia. However, one must understand that the content is also more difficult to control and charge for. Traditional fee-based delivery is not usually an option. Thus, one must plan for different indirect revenues sources such as live performances, service subscriptions, and the sale of enhanced or bundled products. Open content is not a silver bullet that turns services into money making machines. Traditional business models are still valid in many cases.

5. Legal policy is currently not optimal for community created content services. The scope of copyright should be tailored in the future to take into account for example that governments need copyright rarely at all, orphan works should be recyclable, and transformative re-use should be a fundamental user right.

6. Open content licensing projects should work together to create best practice documentation on copyright management issues as a way to limit liabilities. This strategy cannot solve all risks but at least it sets some boundaries on what should not be considered as negligent behavior.

7. Open content licensing needs better interoperability between different licensing projects, and towards copyright collecting societies. It is a major problem for creative collaboration that it is currently impossible to combine works licensed with different "share-alike" -type licenses. Also, other than American recording artists are at disadvantage if their collecting societies refuse them the option to use open content licenses while they continue to collect royalties through the society.

FIGURES

LITERATURE

No creative work is born in isolation. Also the authors of this book have drawn from a number of sources. Parts of the text are based on the authors' prior publications, including:

Hietanen, Herkko and Oksanen, Ville: *"Legal metadata, open content distribution and collecting societies"*, in Bourcier, Danièle and Dulong de Rosnay, Mélanie (eds.): *International Commons at the Digital Age*. Romillat, 2004

Välimäki, Mikko: *The Rise of Open Source Licensing. A Challenge to the Use of Intellectual Property in the Software Industry.* Turre Publishing, 2005

Välimäki, Mikko and Hietanen, Herkko: *"The Challenges of Creative Commons Licensing"*, Computer Law Review 6/2004, pp. 172-177.

In addition to statutes, directives and treaties, the following publications were also frequently consulted and are recommended for further study:

Anderson, Chris: *The Long Tail: Why the Future of Business Is Selling Less of More.* Hyperion, 2006

Benkler, Yochai: *The Wealth of Networks: How Social Production Transforms Markets and Freedom.* Yale University Press, 2006

Best Practices for Online Service Providers. Electronic Frontier Foundation, 2004.

Bourcier, Danièle and Dulong de Rosnay, Mélanie (eds.):
International Commons at the Digital Age. Romillat, 2004

*Documentary Filmmakers' Statement of Best Practices in
Fair Use.* Center for Social Media, 2005

Fischer, William III: *Promises to Keep: Technology, Law, and
the Future of Entertainment.* Stanford University Press, 2004.

Goldstein, Paul: *International Copyright: Principles, Law,
and Practice.* Oxford University Press, 2001.

Gowers Review of Intellectual Property. The Stationery
Office, 2006.

Lerner, Josh and Tirole, Jean: "Some Simple Economics
of Open Source", *Journal of Industrial Economics,* 52
(June 2002), pp. 197-234.

Lessig, Lawrence: *Free Culture.* The Penguin Press, 2004.

Political Influentials in the 2004 Presidential Campaign.
Institute for Politics, Democracy & the Internet, 2004.

Raymond, Eric: *The Cathedral & the Bazaar.* O'Reilly, 2001.

Report on Orphan Works. United States Copyright Office, 2006.

INDEX